Hidden in the Same Mystery:
Thomas Merton and Loretto

# Hidden in the Same Mystery: Thomas Merton and Loretto

Bonnie Thurston, General Editor
Sr. Mary Swain, SL, Loretto Editor
Br. Paul Quenon, OCSO, Gethsemani Photography Editor
Peg Jacobs, CoL, Loretto Photography Editor

FONS VITAE

First published in 2010 by
Fons Vitae
49 Mockingbird Valley Drive
Louisville, KY 40207
http://www.fonsvitae.com
Email: fonsvitaeky@aol.com

Library of Congress Control Number: 2009942558

ISBN 9781891785603

Printed in Canada

# Table of Contents

*Mary Luke Tobin, SL, and Thomas Merton, OCSO, probably early 1960s at Loretto Motherhouse*

*Thomas Merton, Dan Walsh, Luke, and Rose Alma Schuler, SL, probably spring 1968. Rose Alma was Loretto secretary general, 1958-70, when Luke was superior general.*

# Forewords

## Thomas Merton and Sr. Mary Luke Tobin

Thomas Merton and Mary Luke Tobin first met in October of 1960 when Merton brought Dan Walsh over to Loretto to arrange a series of classes by Dan Walsh for the sisters. Merton was immediately taken by Sr. Luke: "energetic, bright, capable, warm, a wonderful person." Mary Luke's response was equally positive: "delightfully simple, very human and very affable." Both were very similar in their simple and direct approach to people. And both were very intent in their pursuit of their vocation and all that it entailed. Bonnie Thurston said that Merton found in Mary Luke "not only an intellectual equal and a woman spiritually in sympathy with his vocation, but a fellow worker for peace and justice." Mary Luke was almost seven years older than Merton, but still close enough in age that they became almost more like brother and sister, each spurring the other on in their respective pursuits.

Merton visited Loretto several times and gave a series of talks and conferences for the sisters. But it was in the private discussions of the two that each profited from the other. With their profound interest in and even zeal for issues of peace, justice, and racism, they stimulated one another in their efforts in these areas. This became even more directly the object of their exchanges when Mary Luke was invited in 1964 to be an official auditor at the final two sessions of the Vatican Council. Mary Luke shared with Merton material that she obtained at the Council, material he often used in contacting various bishops and theologians with his own reflections, particularly on the schema for the Pastoral Constitution on the Church in the Modern World. Merton was especially interested in what the Council would put forward on the issues of nuclear disarmament, peace, and justice.

Merton invited Mary Luke to take part in the two retreats he gave for contemplative sisters in 1967 and 1968. He was interested not only in her presence at these, but in the contributions that she made in the course of the sessions. Those retreats, the contents of which appeared in *The Springs of Contemplation* in 1992, are the closest that Merton and Tobin came to actual collaboration in publication. It would have been very interesting to see what might have come from the two of them working together if Merton had lived longer. Certainly both retained a profound interest and involvement in all of the major issues of our day to the end of their lives.

Mary Luke continued this collaboration, however, even after Merton's death, by fostering her Merton Center in Denver. The last seven years of Mary Luke's life were spent at Loretto. The bond between Merton and Mary Luke, cemented years earlier, had grown into a bond between Gethsemani and Loretto. Each place has maintained close contacts with the other in a way that will go far beyond Merton and Tobin. This is particularly appropriate since the very origins of Gethsemani had close connections with Loretto. It was the Sisters of Loretto who provided the property on which the monks established their foundation. And although it may have taken more than one hundred years before that relationship became more explicit, yet their histories remain closely intertwined. Merton and Gethsemani have profited much from the zeal of Mary Luke and Loretto in areas of peace and justice, renewal of religious life, greater appreciation of the importance of feminism in the Church and in the world at large, as well as the possibility of lay associates as a part of religious life. Loretto has also profited from its contacts with Merton and Gethsemani. This can be seen perhaps particularly in its fostering the contemplative life through its Cedars of Peace and the importance given to the contemplative dimension of the community.

Gethsemani has never adopted a Trappistine community as a part of its connection with the feminine branch of the Cistercian Order. But in many respects Loretto has fulfilled this same goal for the monks. Just as Merton and Mary Luke were more like brother and sister, so the two institutions will remain as brothers and sisters in spirit. We can thank both Merton and Mary Luke for this fact, and trust that they will both continue now from heaven to deepen that relationship even more as both houses of monks and nuns strive to embody and express more fully the full Christ for the world of today.

Fr. James Conner, OCSO

*Academy building, later novitiate building, Loretto Motherhouse*

*Thomas Merton in front of his hermitage*

*Near Badin Pond at Loretto Motherhouse*

# Luke and Merton

When her international ecumenical work on the staff of Church Women United took her to Thailand in 1974, Mary Luke Tobin had the opportunity for a brief visit to the center near Bangkok where Thomas Merton had died. Later she would comment that the little cottage, then occupied by a small family, bore no sign proclaiming, "Here is where a great monk, a great writer died." Perhaps that observation describes Luke's relationship with Merton.

Their initial meeting, detailed elsewhere in this book, was not that of a follower seeking an audience with an admired hero, but an occasion for Merton's job-hunting for his former professor. Luke, always grateful for her contacts with Merton during the last eight years of his life, looked upon him as one with whom she could exchange ideas and from whom she could seek advice. Luke once said that never did she think, "Here's this great person whose presence I'm in." Rather, she appreciated the qualities which made him so approachable, so affable, describing him as "just a good, warm, and terribly insightful friend."

His reflections on prayer, commitment, and religious life were shared with her, with Loretto novices, and with small groups of sisters, including Luke's colleagues in administration and those responsible for training young religious. Merton visited the Loretto Motherhouse for occasional talks and to consult with Luke. In turn, she was invited to Gethsemani, especially after the sessions of the Second Vatican Council where she was an auditor, to update the monks on developments at that historic gathering. Merton himself was always eager to hear her reports about the Council. She sought his opinion about the new guidelines for the Loretto Congregation being drawn up as part of the nascent renewal of religious life. In honor of Loretto's sesquicentennial in 1962, Merton wrote an essay on "Loretto and Gethsemani." Luke was the recipient of several of Merton's mimeographed essays, especially those on peace circulated privately to friends at a time when he was forbidden to publish his ideas on that topic.

After moving to the hermitage, Merton, eager to share that experience with her, at first sent her photographs of it, and eventually, in 1967, received permission for her to visit it. Luke, recalling the book-filled shelves and Merton's description of his solitary life of writing, reading, and going to the woods, commented, "I believe what he wanted to indicate was that the life of the mind and the life of prayer were well integrated for him. And he had found the ideal place to experience both."

Merton's insights into the issues of racism, the Vietnam War, the spread of nuclear weapons, resonated with Luke's growing concern about crucial world problems. She admired the courage and wisdom which inspired his grappling with them, often commenting on how Merton, a true visionary back in the 1960s, wrote with keen prescience on topics such as deterrence and pre-emptive first strikes, ideas connected with the rise of nuclearism in the 1980s.

Luke's recollections of her personal contacts with Merton as well as her intense study of his writings provided the material for her frequent lectures as well as for seminary and summer classes on Merton. In addition to founding the Thomas Merton Center for Creative Exchange in Denver, treated elsewhere in this book, and later collaborating in the formation of the International Thomas Merton Society, Luke traveled the country to share the challenging ideas she had learned from Merton. A clipping file holds articles about her Merton talks from newspapers in locations as varied as Kansas City, Louisville, Salt Lake City, Los Angeles, St. Louis, New York City, and Milwaukee.

As an adjunct professor at Denver's Iliff School of Theology (a Methodist-founded seminary), Luke taught several short-term and summer courses on Merton. The syllabus for one, entitled "Creating a Community of Justice, and the Spirituality of Thomas Merton," offered appendices that included an interview with Luke on Merton and prayer; the text of a tape in which Merton recorded his dialogic reflections while listening to a black jazz player; an excerpt from *Conjectures of a Guilty Bystander*, recounting the Fourth and Walnut epiphany; three Merton reflections on prayer; Merton's conditions for Christian nonviolence; his poem, "Macarius and the Pony;" an excerpt from Daniel Berrigan on Merton; "The Wild Places," an essay showing his concern for Earth.

For fifteen consecutive summers, 1982-1996, Luke was one of the guest lecturers at Ring Lake Ranch, a rustic retreat center in Wyoming, where with few exceptions her two-week sessions were always on Merton. Some of the course titles illustrate her various approaches to his thought: "Themes of Struggle and Hope in Thomas Merton," "Prayer and Prophecy in Thomas Merton," "The Desert Experience: A Journey with Thomas Merton," "Thomas Merton: Spirituality and Action."

When asked in the early 1980s to describe her contemporary faith development for a *Journeys in Faith* series of books, Luke wrote *Hope Is an Open Door,* including a chapter on Merton's influence on her work for renewal in religious life and her commitment to justice and peace activity.

While her published writing about Merton was very limited, Luke for many years was especially eager that a certain set of retreat talks given by him should become available to readers. In December 1967 and again in May 1968, Merton had invited her to participate in gatherings of some contemplative prioresses which he hosted at Gethsemani. Remembering the richness of those sessions, Luke worked persistently to bring them to print. She obtained tape recordings of the meetings, had typed transcripts made of them, engaged a skilled editor, negotiating all the while with those in key roles in the realm of Merton publication. Finally, in 1992, the proceedings appeared in *The Springs of Contemplation: A Retreat at the Abbey of Gethsemani*. The present book will doubtlessly be a posthumous tribute to Luke's deep desire that Merton's talks to Loretto novices be shared widely.

For the PBS documentary, *Merton,* Luke was one of twenty friends and acquaintances of the Trappist to be interviewed. Later, editor Paul Wilkes gathered the conversations into an intriguing collection of reminiscences, *Merton By Those Who Knew Him Best.* Perhaps the final paragraph of Luke's commentary succinctly describes her relationship to Merton: "I appreciate having had the pleasure of knowing him, the delight of having him come into a room, smiling, welcoming, filled with interest about everything in the world, looking for my response. Who could help but love this man? He never was a 'guru' to me, but rather a good friend with whom I could exchange ideas, and I value that greatly."

Sr. Cecily Jones, SL

# The Genesis

In May of 2001 I visited Sister Mary Luke Tobin at her Motherhouse in Loretto, Kentucky. Luke and I had worked together with many others to found the International Thomas Merton Society, and we had been on a number of Merton programs together. She had invited me to Denver on several occasions to speak at the Thomas Merton Center for Creative Exchange which she founded. We were "dharma friends" in Thomas Merton. That spring visit, Luke gave me Xerox copies of the following talks in the hopes that they could be published as a book. She wanted me to shepherd that volume into being. Subsequently, in March 2002, through the kindness of Sister Rose Annette Liddell, SL, I made contact in Denver with Sister Mary Catherine Rabbitt, SL, then President of the Loretto Community, to secure her permission to proceed with the project. It was granted in June 2002. The next step was to secure permission of the Merton Legacy Trust to print this Merton material. This took from August to the end of September 2002, and would not have happened without the kind assistance of Anne McCormick of the Trust. In November and December 2002, I was in correspondence with a university press about publishing the work as well as seeking further Merton material from the Loretto archives. (None was forthcoming.) After the press contact fizzled in the winter of 2003, the project lay dormant on my desk until the spring of 2004 when Rose Annette Liddell lit a fire under me about it, and Sister Mary Swain, SL, picked up the torch for Loretto.

What follows in Part I, then, are the four texts of Merton's talks that Luke entrusted to me with the addition of some framing material, Merton's essay, "Loretto and Gethsemani," and a note on the Merton-Tobin correspondence. First there is a brief essay introducing Merton's friendship with Sister Luke, Merton's life and thought from 1961-1963, the years these talks cover, and transcripts of the talks themselves. I have reproduced the talks verbatim from the transcripts Luke gave me, changing only the punctuation (to standardize it) and nothing else. Capitalization and paragraphing are as they appear in the transcripts as are the headings. I have taken the liberty of providing a brief introduction for each of the talks and annotating with footnotes a few of Merton's references. With the help of Patricia A. Burton's invaluable *Merton Vade Mecum* (1998 edition),[1] I was able to place each talk in the context of Merton's writing and with the help of Merton's journals for 1960-1963[2] (edited by Victor Kramer) I could place the talks in the context of Merton's day-to-day life.

In style the material in these talks is like that found in Merton's talks to the novices at Gethsemani: informal, rambling (even disorganized), but full of sharp insights, especially into religious life and the life of prayer. (As it has developed, prayer has become the theme of this little book.) These talks are precursors to Merton's talks to the Trappistines at Our Lady of the Redwoods in California, the Precious Blood Sisters in Alaska,[3] and somewhat earlier in 1967 and 1968 the contemplative prioresses' meetings held at Gethsemani which were facilitated by the Loretto Sisters and especially Sister Luke. Sister Jane Marie Richardson, SL, has already provided us with the wonderful collection of Merton's talks to the prioresses, *The Springs of Contemplation*.[4] That volume contains the essay Merton wrote for the Sisters of Loretto in the spring of 1962 as they celebrated the 150th anniversary of their congregation. It is an important piece of the history of "Merton and Loretto," a history that is yet to be completely researched and written and which I hope someone will undertake. I suspect there is more Merton and Loretto material out there with which the Sisters of Loretto, as did the sisters who preserved the now classic work of Jean-Pierre de Caussade, may yet gift us.

My special thanks and immense respect and affection go to Sister Mary Luke, Sister Rose Annette Liddell, and Sister Mary Swain for their confidence, patience (especially patience) and friendship. Thanks to Br. Paul Quenon, OCSO, and Gray Henry for the beautiful art work and to Anne McCormick of the Merton Legacy Trust without whom, nothing.

Bonnie Thurston
General Editor
Ash Wednesday, 2009

Endnotes

1. Patricia A. Burton, *Merton Vade Mecum: A Road-Map for Readers* (Louisville, KY: Thomas Merton Foundation, 1998).

2. Victor A. Kramer, ed., *Turning Toward the World: The Journals of Thomas Merton* Volume Four 1960-1963 (San Francisco: Harper San Francisco, 1997).

3. The Alaskan conferences are published in their entirety in *Thomas Merton in Alaska* (New York: New Directions, 1988).

4. Jane Marie Richardson, ed., *The Springs of Contemplation: A Retreat at the Abbey of Gethsemani* (New York: Farrar, Straus, Giroux, 1992).

*Mary statue with turtle and quote from "Loretto and Gethsemani"*

*We are not only neighbors in a valley that is still lonely, but we are equally the children of exile and of revolution. Perhaps this is a good reason why we are both hidden in the same mystery of Our Lady's Sorrow and Solitude in the Lord's Passion.*

Part I: Thomas Merton: Writings for Loretto

*Abbey of Gethsemani church*

*Inside the monastery*

# Introduction

We are not only neighbors in a valley that is still lonely, but we are equally the children of exile and of revolution. Perhaps this is a good reason why we are both hidden in the same mystery of Our Lady's Sorrow and Solitude in the Lord's Passion.[1]

So begins the essay which Thomas Merton wrote to commemorate the 150th anniversary of the founding of the Loretto Community, a community of religious women he loved, with whom he had sustained and sustaining contact, and to whom the following talks were given.

The Sisters of Loretto and the Trappists of Our Lady of Gethsemani Abbey were in conversation long before the mid-twentieth century when Sr. Mary Luke Tobin invited Fr. Thomas Merton to give talks to the sisters in her community. In 1805 a Belgian priest, Fr. Charles Nerinckx, arrived in Kentucky and quickly became friends with the Dant family in Nelson County. In 1812, at the request of a Dant cousin, Mary Rhodes, he wrote a religious rule for a community of women. That rule is foundational for the Sisters of Loretto at the Foot of the Cross, Kentucky's first religious foundation. In March 1818, six Loretto Sisters opened a school on property donated to them by the Dant family. They called it "Gethsemani." In 1847 the sisters decided to sell the Dant property. Fr. Paulinus of the Abbey of Melleray near Nantes was looking for property for a Trappist foundation in America. He bought the property of 1,500 acres from the sisters for about $5,000, and in 1848 a Trappist community of 44 brothers from France made their foundation there. It is the community that we now know as Our Lady of Gethsemani, the home of Thomas Merton.[2]

Mary Luke Tobin entered Loretto in 1927, took perpetual vows in 1932 and became superior general of the Sisters of Loretto in 1958, a position she held until 1970. She was elected president of the Conference of Major Superiors of Women in 1964 and was an official American woman auditor at the Second Vatican Council, together with Catherine McCarthy, president of the National Council of Catholic Women, and Sister Claudia Feddish, superior general of the Sisters of St. Basil the Great (Pennsylvania), a Byzantine rite congregation. In particular she was on the subcommittee on Schema Thirteen, the commission for the document on the Church in the Modern World, about which she frequently corresponded[3] and consulted with Merton.[4] She was one of Merton's "inside sources" on the work of Vatican II. Indeed, practically from the beginning of her tenure as superior at Loretto, Sr. Luke and Thomas Merton were friends. Michael Mott aptly notes that "the atmosphere at the convent delighted [Merton], and he had come to find in Mother Luke a kindred spirit."[5] And I would add, an intellect on a par with his own. They were both passionately interested in the renewal of religious life, in peace and social justice issues, and in the intersection of the two. They remained close friends until Merton's death in 1968.[6]

Sr. Luke reports that in 1960 Merton traveled the twelve miles from Gethsemani to Loretto to see if his friend and former Columbia University professor, Dan Walsh, might teach at the Loretto Sisters' junior college. Luke says, "We were the ideal place for that...."[7] Subsequently, Sr. Luke invited Merton to give talks to the novices and other groups of sisters at Loretto, invitations Merton apparently happily accepted as they gave him access to a community he enjoyed and to stimulating (and I venture to say sustaining) talks with Luke, herself. What Merton wrote of the connection between the Kentucky Trappists and Loretto also, to some degree, describes his personal relationship to the community: "it is a quiet mixture of wisdom and madness, a triumph of hope over despair. ... we have both descended from ancestors who died accomplishing the impossible. Or rather from people who accepted as perfectly normal the incongruity and solitude which are the lot of the pioneer."[8] Certainly Merton's reflections on his visits to Loretto are in evidence in his journals[9] and are mentioned in many of his letters.

The transcripts which follow are of the talks which were all given in the early 1960s. It was, to say the least, a turbulent time in the United States and the world. The threat of nuclear war and the Cold War shrouded the human family. In 1961 America was reeling from the Bay of Pigs invasion. The Vietnam War was escalating, and in March 1961 the United States government admitted U.S. forces were engaging in combat missions. In the United States, the civil rights movement was picking up steam; 1963 saw both the "Letter from the Birmingham Jail" and the "I Have a Dream" speech by Dr. Martin Luther King, Jr. In November of that year President Kennedy was assassinated. The specter of nuclear holocaust, the Cuban missile crisis, Vietnam and civil rights form the political backdrop of these talks. On October 11, 1962, the Second Vatican Council was convened, and persons as intelligent as Sr. Luke and Merton certainly understood the profound changes that would follow. Indeed, they were at the forefront of many of them.

Nor was it a placid time for Merton, himself. His journals in the early 1960s indicate increasing dis-ease at Gethsemani and a longing for more solitude than his life in the community allowed. Additionally, he was deeply concerned about issues of war and peace and civil rights in America. He began what have come to be known as the "Cold War Letters" in 1961. He had written so much on these issues[10] that on January 20, 1962, the Abbot General of the Cistercians wrote Dom James Fox at Gethsemani requiring Merton to cease publication on issues of war and peace.[11] Merton's journal entries during the community's retreat, January 19-25, 1962, are characteristic of his state of mind at the time. Between 1961 and 1963 Merton prepared for publication and/or published *The New Man, New Seeds of Contemplation, Life and Holiness* as well as the volumes of verse *Original Child Bomb* and *Emblems of a Season of Fury*. In addition to the many letters and journal entries, there are important periodical articles, and, in particular, the "Root of War" article in *The Catholic Worker* in 1961. Certainly in the early 1960s Merton was "turning toward the world" again, after his "honeymoon period" in monastic life. After 20 years, he knew both sides of religious profession and, as Sr. Luke so wisely understood, was well placed to address the Sisters of Loretto on matters that would affect both their lives of prayer and of public witness...which both Luke and Merton knew to be the same life.

As noted earlier, these talks are in style similar to those he gave to his own novices. They deal with matters related to religious life and the life of prayer, subjects which are treated at greater and more systematic length elsewhere, but especially in the essays collected in *The Monastic Journey*[12] and in *Contemplation in a World of Action*.[13]

## Endnotes

1. Thomas Merton, "Loretto and Gethsemani." Essay written by Merton in commemoration of the 150th anniversary of the founding of the Congregation of the Sisters of Loretto at the Foot of the Cross, p. 3 of the original booklet edition.

2. For more on the history see Dianne Aprile, *The Abbey of Gethsemani: Place of Peace and Paradox* (Louisville: Trout Lily Press, 1998); Thomas Merton, "Loretto and Gethsemani," 1962 (an essay reprinted in Jane Marie Richardson's *The Springs of Contemplation*, 1992 and also in this volume); Christine Bochen, "Loretto and Gethsemani" in William H. Shannon et al., *The Thomas Merton Encyclopedia* (Maryknoll: Orbis Press, 2002), 267-268.

3. See, for example, the eight letters to Sr. Luke in Br. Patrick Hart, ed., *Thomas Merton, The School of Charity: Letters on Religious Renewal and Spiritual Direction* (New York: Farrar, Straus, Giroux, 1990).

4. For more on Sr. Luke see William Shannon, "Tobin, Mary Luke" in *The Thomas Merton Encyclopedia*, 488-489; her own book, *Hope Is an Open Door* (Nashville: Abingdon, 1981); and Elizabeth McCloskey, "More Than a Footnote: The Footprints of Mary Luke Tobin at Vatican II," *The Merton Seasonal* 32.2 (Summer 2007) 10-34.

5. Michael Mott, *The Seven Mountains of Thomas Merton* (Boston: Houghton

Mifflin, 1984), 410.

6. An indication of this closeness is that at the height of his relationship with the student nurse, on July 13, 1966, Merton and Jim Wygal went to Loretto, but Luke was away. One wonders what might have transpired had Merton had the advantage of this wise woman's counsel. See Mott, 447 and Merton's journal entry for July 14, 1966, in Christine M. Bochen, ed., *Learning to Love: The Journals of Thomas Merton* Volume Six 1966-1967 (San Francisco: Harper San Francisco, 1997), 95.

7. Paul Wilkes, ed., *Merton By Those Who Knew Him Best* (San Francisco: Harper and Row, 1984), 95. And see the whole interview with Sr. Luke, 94-99.

8. Merton, "Loretto and Gethsemani," 5.

9. See, in particular, Victor Kramer, ed., *Turning Toward the World: The Journals of Thomas Merton* Volume Four 1960-1963 (San Francisco: Harper San Francisco, 1997).

10. Thomas Merton, *Cold War Letters*, ed. William H. Shannon and Christine M. Bouchen (Maryknoll, NY: Orbis, 2006).

11. Kramer, ed. 194-198. The full manuscript on these subjects which he prepared in 1962, *Peace in the Post-Christian Era*, was not published until 2004. Patricia A Burton, ed., *Thomas Merton: Peace in the Post-Christian Era* (Maryknoll, NY: Orbis Books, 2004).

12. Br. Patrick Hart, ed., *The Monastic Journey* (Kansas City: Sheed Andrew and McMeel, Inc., 1977).

13. Thomas Merton, *Contemplation in a World of Action* (Garden City, NY: Doubleday, 1971).

# October 4, 1961, Loretto Junior College

## Introductory Note

Although the notes on the conference Merton gave are brief, the event clearly moved him. His journal entry for October 5, 1961, is largely devoted to his visit to Loretto the previous day.[1] He notes that he had "begged off" attending Loretto's Sesquicentennial, but enjoyed this private visit which "turned into a celebration nevertheless."[2] The postulants and novices sang a musical program on the history of Loretto which focused on the Westward movement of their pioneering community. Merton was touched by the young women, "the wide-eyed, disoriented look of the new postulants."[3] He reports he spoke a little to the novices and postulants, in the infirmary, and then with Mother Luke and her council. The notes which follow are apparently from the talk to the novices. Merton reports he had dinner in the guesthouse and "laughed a great deal."[4] Merton noted, "Never anywhere, even at the Louisville Carmel, have I felt so much at home, so much with real friends with whom there could be a complete and unreserved understanding, at least about the religious life and its problems. The wonderful, salutary honesty of Loretto and of Mother Luke! This is a treasure beyond estimation."[5]

On October 9, 1961, Merton wrote to Sister Helen Jean Seidel, SL, mistress of novices at Loretto, "enclosing a few copies of the notes on mental prayer I have given to the novices. There is nothing much to them, but they may serve a purpose. Then too a lot of things could be said to clarify the rather jumbled thought I was giving out the other day."[6] He continues by clarifying his thoughts on mental prayer, stressing the necessity for real training in the form and for the importance of not clinging too closely to any set of rules for the practice. The letter as printed closes "I wish I had had a few more minutes with the novices and postulants: they gave me much more than I was able to give them. But I certainly enjoyed it."[7]

The transcript of the October 4th talk begins with the following paragraph: *"Father Louis began speaking by thanking the novices and postulants for a beautiful performance of the Cantata, 'We Give You Glory,' using references to 'Wagons Roll West' and 'Bienvenidas, Hermanas,' as points of departure for the remainder of what he said."* Then what is apparently the transcript of Merton's words begins. There is no indication in the transcript of the difference between this "framing" and Merton's words. I have added it here for clarity's sake.

## Merton's Talk

I like very much the idea of New Mexico; it is a tremendous thing to work with the Indians. The Indians have something we have lost over the centuries, a contact with reality. The Indians still, to a great extent you will find (like the Hopis, for example) have this tremendous sense of something that we have lost, this sense of nature as made by and coming from God. It would be good for you, as sisters, to see some of that, to hear the something they have to say to you about God.

I could go on forever about the Indians, but I would like to talk to you about vocation, your vocation. Religious life is a vocation, not a job. A job is something you do; vocation is something completely personal and supernatural. But when we say supernatural we don't mean that it is different, but that it is something just between God and us. It is not just something above nature; it is divine, a personal relationship with God. From the moment that you start you are a different person. Your life will never be the same, for you have been spoken to by God. You now have a responsibility and a privilege which is unique, for the world is full of people who have never been spoken to by God. You belong in a special rank.

Don't ever think of your vocation as being an uncertainty, as "I have not made vows yet." God has spoken to you! And since you have given yourself to Him in answer to His call you should feel no insecurity whatsoever about your relationship with Him. From the moment that anyone has heard God's voice in his heart he was a saint.[8] What matters is that God has taken possession of us; and He cannot leave us, even if we "get tough" about it.

But don't think of God only as the strong and the mighty, and don't think of yourself in His power, but think of Him in your power. Remember that it is Himself and not just His life that He has given you—so that God depends on you for His life in you. He has given Himself to us, to man weak and frail, giving us a little flame of life in Himself.

There should be in our relation a feeling of tender love which implies a sense of tenderness toward the littleness of God in everyone. As Sisters you have a tremendous amount to do with a child's becoming aware of this presence of God in him. The worst thing that can happen to a child is to be led out of that spontaneous relation with God's power in him that he possesses in his innocence.

Today we are bombarded with appeals to be aggressive. However, it is not aggressive that we have to be. You have to be humble, that is the Gospel. Our Lord has said not to assert self. Every time you do you create crosses for yourself and others.

The world today is full of people who are scared to death. We are in danger now because no one can settle down. We felt that we had to stay tough after something like the Atomic Bomb. But it is not being tough and laying down the law that matters. It is rather a question of appreciating the value of littleness. And you must begin by doing this among yourselves. Appreciate your own weakness; don't get mad at yourself for a failure. We are supposed to do things wrong (not on purpose!). Our mistakes give us the power of appreciating others' mistakes. We can more easily forgive one another in the knowledge, realization and appreciation of the weakness in all men.

The greatest of all powers is to be little and small and weak. For was not the manifestation of God in the world that of weakness—the Cross? God willed so to manifest His power. Power is made perfect in failure.[9] The good that is in the world is not coming from great people but from very small people. I am quite sure that if Mary were to appear in our country it would most certainly be among the Indians, or Negroes, or Puerto Ricans—not on Park Avenue.[10]

## Endnotes

1. Victor A. Kramer, ed., *Turning Toward the World: The Journals of Thomas Merton* Volume Four 1960-1963 (San Francisco: Harper San Francisco, 1997), 167-169.

2. Ibid., 167-168.

3. Ibid., 168.

4. Ibid.

5. Ibid.

6. In Br. Patrick Hart, ed., *Thomas Merton, The School of Charity: Letters on Religious Renewal and Spiritual Direction* (New York: Harcourt, Brace, Jovanovich, 1990), 140.

7. Hart, 141.

8. Thomas Merton did not use inclusive language. I have heard Sister Luke Tobin say on many occasions that he would have come to this inclusive usage. But in the 1960s he used the masculine pronoun for all human beings and for the deity. I have retained its use throughout these talks for the sake of historical accuracy.

9. The reference is to 2 Corinthians 12:9, part of a longer passage dealing with power and weakness.

10. Merton uses this image of Park Avenue in his essay for the Loretto anniversary commemoration. There it is the image of all the Loretto sisters are *not* to be. He contrasts Park Avenue with the foot of the cross, a powerful comparison for the Sisters of Loretto at the Foot of the Cross.

# Father Louis' Talk to Second-Year Novices
## January 10, 1962

### Introductory Note

Merton has journal entries for January 9 and 12, 1962, neither of which mentions his visit to Loretto.[1] The entry for January 12, 1962, mentions his visit to the Methodist Seminary at Asbury to which he alludes in the following talk. The journal entries of late December and early January indicate that Merton was thinking about Julian of Norwich (December 25 and 27), Sufi mystics (January 3) and the Shakers (January 3, 12).[2] The community of Gethsemani began a retreat on January 19. On January 20 the Abbot General wrote to Dom James to silence Merton's writing on war and peace.

Interestingly, on May 29, 1962, Merton wrote to Sister Luke and enclosed a "little letter I wrote to the vow class."[3] Merton's note to those about-to-be-professed novices is printed in its entirety in *Witness to Freedom* and follows in this collection. In it he speaks to them again of self-giving and of belonging to Christ, and, again, he asks for their prayers and promises them his own.

The transcript of the talk itself contains questions from Merton and the group's response, here printed in italic for the sake of clarity.

### Merton's Talk

You're the class that's going to make vows, is that right?
*Yes, Father—on Ascension Thursday.*[4]

I was ordained on Ascension Thursday. I guess when you make your vows on that day you'll all be able to rise again with Christ. But you know, you don't have to rise; you don't have to go anywhere. St. Paul says: Who should bring Him down from Heaven or bring Him up from the depths? No, the Word is very near. It is in our hearts,[5] and that's the reason you don't have to ascend, because heaven is on earth. Heaven is in our hearts since Christ is in our hearts. And that is one of the great things to realize, that you don't have to go anywhere much in order to find Our Lord. We don't have to find Him because He comes to find us, you see; that is what we must remember most of all; we find Him by letting Him find us. And I suppose that is what the vows are. You make vows, but, actually, it is by your vows that He takes possession of you, and so it is more His work than it is yours, actually.

Funny thing, when I was over at Asbury there, talking to these Methodist ministers, one of them spoke about having met an ex-Trappist novice from Georgia on a train somewhere, and about having ridden a couple of hours on the train talking with this ex-Trappist, and having had a very interesting conversation. The ex-novice got very confidential.[6] And one of the things he said was that at one point he went to the monastery to be a saint, and at a certain point, he said, "I got to feeling I was almost there." And I said: "Yeah, he was out of the monastery, wasn't he?"

That is the way it goes, you see. This business of feeling that sanctity is just around the corner is a great delusion. That isn't the way it's supposed to be, you see. We should not live in that dimension at all, going along a horizontal line where you are always looking for something that is going to turn up, and you are just going to reach it. It is like the carrot in front of the donkey, and the donkey keeps going and never gets the carrot. Some people want the spiritual life to be that way. It is not supposed to be that way. You are always ahead of yourself. You never catch up to where you really belong, which is right where you are, you see. And you are always outside of yourself, and it is to be alienated from yourself, to be away from where Christ is.

It is not that we are going to have Christ with us tomorrow; we have Him with us now. And it is because we have Him now that we will have Him tomorrow, and not the other way around. Instead of looking for some wonderful day or time when it will all open up, just realize that we don't have to wait. In a certain sense, from the moment that we have completely surrendered ourselves to Him, we have arrived, not in heaven, of course, but in the Church, in our place in the Church; we have arrived where we belong. If we are where we belong nothing else matters. If we have to be brought somewhere, then He will bring us where we have to be brought. We don't have to plan our journey anymore; we just do what He says. Once you get on the train you just stay on until you get to your station.

Really, the whole institution of vows is to make life very simple for us. Because when we have our vows, if we are living our vows, we are where we belong; you see, we are on the train. That is the whole point of vows, it is so you know very clearly where you are. You can always tell what the will of God is, and you have no particular problem about that. And so the great thing when you have your vows is that you don't have to worry too much about where you are going. You just do what you do.

If you don't have vows it is harder to do that. It takes more faith. And, in a way, you can say that vows make a life of faith much easier, you see, and right before your nose all day long you have what you know you have to do to please God. Whereas, if you don't have vows, it's a whole lot harder. You have to look around. But in all life there is uncertainty. Vows will not take away all uncertainty and will not take away all risk.

One thing comes to mind. Maybe the Holy Spirit wants me to say this. With the vow of obedience...what is one of the greatest difficulties of the vow of obedience?—not the vow itself, but let's say the virtue of obedience.[7] One of the greatest difficulties in the virtue of obedience comes when you have been in religion a little while, and you get into jobs, and you become very conscientiously involved in works you have to do for your community and work for your order, and Superiors make decisions about your works that lead in a direction you don't desire. And here is the thing that is hard, when you know that something is not coming from the Superior but from other religious who are on the same level as you and who have worked on the Superior to move the thing in that direction. This is very hard. This is a temptation you will run into; it makes life very difficult. We have it much more in our Order where we are all together and everybody, when they don't have anything else to do, they go tell the Superior how to run the monastery (a favorite sport of Trappist monks). And everybody may feel that it is very fine for something to be done in a certain way and an eager-beaver goes and persuades the Superior to do it in a completely different way, and everybody has to take it, knowing that it doesn't come from the Superior but it comes from Father "X." That is sometimes a little difficult.

But now how are we going to handle a thing like that? If you get all excited about two different ways of doing things (you've got your way and Sister "X's") and Sister "X" has sold the Superior the idea of doing it her way, there is only one way of handling that and that is to see that neither way matters much. It is not so much a question of offering it up and making an enormous sacrifice of it, saying, "This is the end! I'll do this! I wouldn't do it in this way, but over my dead body it's being done!" But it is rather a question of seeing that neither way is terribly important. Supposing it is done Sister "X's" way, does it make that much difference? Do you really care that much? Sometimes our greatest temptations with regard to obedience come from the delusion that we really care that much about how a thing ought to be done. If we looked into our inmost heart we would find that we really didn't care and that it didn't matter that much to us.

Say the Superior tells us to do something that seems to us to be tragic. It doesn't have to be tragic. We may feel that it's tragic at the moment, but it isn't our true self that feels like that; it is a kind of a self that we develop in community life, a self we develop in self-defense. It isn't our real self and that is the self that causes most of the trouble. So when you say that by your vows you have to renounce yourself, you certainly do have to renounce all of yourself, but you have to first and most truly renounce your superficial self, the one that thinks it is very excited and really isn't. It is very important in religious life to realize that we are not as excited as we imagine about a lot of things which we seem to be excited about on the surface, because deep down we are much more involved in things which are more important. But they are things which we can't talk about. The things we get excited about are things we can communicate very easily, and because we can communicate them, we can form words about them immediately in our mind; we can phrase sentences about it; we can formulate arguments about why it is bad or why it is good. Well, the things we can talk about, the things we can explain, are usually the least important things in our lives, and they take us away from the deeper things about which we can say nothing. You don't even understand them clearly. Those are the real things in our life and the things which we can't understand very well, and the things we can't talk about. So very often what it amounts to is we just get upset about something. We must drop that and get back to the thing which is more important in our soul which we don't understand. Deeper than the thing which I get all excited about is a deeper thing which I can't get excited about because I have not really grasped it. That is much more important.

The sacrifices that we get in the life of the vows are for that. They are supposed to take us off the level where everything is cut and dried, because on that level anything can happen. You are liable to have to drop anything at any moment. But the deeper things of life you never have to drop; they're never going to be taken away from you. This is the Mary-Martha bit.[8] On the level of Martha you can always be choosing between this and that. Martha is solicitous about many things, all of them equally good or equally indifferent—they don't matter that much. And to be solicitous about many things is to be solicitous about things that don't matter; they only matter relatively. There is one thing that matters, and it can't be taken away. Not that it's a question of action or contemplation; it is neither one. It is deeper; it is your soul united to God, God present in your soul. It is His will in you. Nobody can touch that; nobody can do anything to that; nobody can harm it in the least bit—even yourself in a certain way. God is not going to let you hurt yourself in a deep way. He'll let you fool around on a superficial level; He'll let you make life complicated and miserable for yourself, if you like. It is not really important at all. Some people have to do that or they wouldn't have anything to think about at all. But even though we may complicate our lives through our own fault, it doesn't affect the deep work that God is doing in our hearts.

One spiritual writer I would like to recommend to you—you probably never read her—it's a very good friend of mine called Lady Julian of

Norwich.[9] A lot of her stuff is in an ancient English style. She and Cardinal Newman[10] are two of the great English theologians. She is a fourteenth-century contemplative who lived as a recluse in a little house attached to a church which had a window through which she received communion. And her whole life is built on some revelations, basic revelations of the mercy of God which she had in her youth and a theological development of what is contained in that revelation. That is to say, there are certain basic things which are truths of faith and certain reasoning which she carried on to elucidate these things. And the basic thing in her is a kind of attempt to solve the contradiction in her mind that arose as a result of this revelation. On the one hand was the teaching, the traditional teaching, about sin and the constant threat and danger of sin, and how a person is constantly in a state just on the edge of the abyss. And there is that traditional mentality that sin is a terrible thing. But Our Lord said that, "yeah, that's true, but that is not the way it is." It is true! But the thing that He revealed to her was that "while all this is going on I am doing something else. While you are in danger, I am your salvation. You can worry about your danger if you want to (it's not necessary to worry about it, but if you want to worry go ahead and worry), but I will make all things well."

And Julian said: "What about all these souls that fall into Hell?"

"Mind your own business! You do not know what I am doing with all those people. How do you know they are in Hell? Who told you they were in Hell? I make all things well. I make all things come out right."

She said: "How do we know this?"

He said: "You don't know this. There is going to be a day for which I have reserved my great deed, when I will show how I make all things well. You will see it then, but now you don't see it."

What time is it? Are you to have supper at 5:15? 5:00? Which is it?

*5:25, Father.*

Oh, well, we have plenty of time. Do you have any questions? Last time I was here you didn't get a chance to ask any questions. Now that we have a little time maybe you would like to ask some. Do you want me to talk about anything else? How about the rest of the vows?

*Vows!*

We will say that this was obedience.

Chastity. Well, that again—there's one where you might worry. Chastity is the worrying vow; it's the one that causes the most headaches over the least, actually. We have to take a very positive view of what chastity is about, and I think probably that should be easier for you as women because the real meaning of the vow of chastity is consecration as a bride of Christ. It's not so easy for us to think in terms of "bride of Christ." It's much easier for you; it's natural for you, and I think that this should make things much easier and simple as far as understanding the vow of chastity goes. Because if you are the spouse of Christ, He will certainly make all things well. That idea of that particular, wonderful relationship with Our Lord of a totally consecrated heart that belongs completely to Him is the solution to all problems because, you see, His love for us is so great that He can't be moved by our failings, can't be moved to anger against us by our little involuntary failings. I think your chastity should be a source of confidence; the very relationship which it brings you to with Our Lord should be a source of very great confidence that, even though you may have temptations, these should bring you closer to Him. He loves those who suffer and are tempted; He loves people who have a hard time. If you were married outside, in married life instead of in religion, you would have a hard time. And hard times are supposed to make marriages more solid. It is a very great tragedy today that the things which are supposed to make marriage solid are the things that break it up. That is because of the weakness and the ignorance of human beings.

We are totally ignorant of life today. People have no sense of what life is about any more. Probably one of the reasons for that is that, in a society where there is so much advertising, and where people are always constantly presented with a funny image of life, and in which people are always supremely happy because they have just bought a new car, or just bought a new TV or something, you get that image that happiness is very easy to have; you just buy *this*. And, therefore, happiness is accessible to all, and if there is the slightest unhappiness or something so radically wrong that you can't do anything about it, except buy something else (and you can't really do it by buying things), and so they give up trying.

People are led to despair by the so-called "advertising industry" because of the image that it creates of this false happiness. And so marriages are probably wrecked in many cases by the picture that a husband or wife gets, the image that is created in their minds of these mythical people that are always happy, that are created by these advertisements.

Well, now, we of all people should be as unlike that as possible. We should realize that in our union with Christ it's a union for better or for worse—and there's a lot of worse on our side. But it doesn't matter; He wants to take those things upon Himself. He doesn't want to be reproaching us all the time; He is our physician. If there is something which has to be healed, He is our physician. When He healed the lepers[11] He didn't first of all give them a lecture about what dirty lepers they were; or the poor woman who touched the hem of His garment;[12] she was so ashamed. But He didn't reproach her for that; He was glad that she did that.

These are the things which we have to remember. Above all, do not let chastity become a source of worry. It is possible to have all kinds of deep interior anguish about this question of chastity, but it should never be thought of as in the least an obstacle, should never be thought of as a barrier between you and Our Lord. That is the way the devil tries to separate you from your source of strength, and so the only thing that we can say about chastity is, let everything, no matter what it is, temptation or what else, drive you to Him. Chastity has separated you from any other refuge. By the vow of chastity we have given up the refuge the people have in the world. If a person in the world is tempted, he can get married. But the vow of chastity if you are tempted you have only one refuge, which is Christ. You have given everything else up. So then you just go to Him.

Poverty. That is, in a certain way, the most important of the vows today. It is a crucial vow today. It is the real test of our religious life, and it is a test in which we fail. It is a test in which I fail. There we should worry a bit. With chastity we should not worry; with poverty we should worry. With poverty we've got reason to worry. We are not poor! We are rich; we are comfortable; we have everything! If we go to a hospital we get the nicest room; people treat us well wherever we go. Sometimes we don't even have to pay in a hospital. As priests and religious we have everything.

And you especially are liable to go among people that have absolutely nothing. And the majority of the people in the world have nothing, and the great problem of the world today is the whole question of having and not having. The world is turned upside down by having and not having, by the torment that is caused to the millions of people who have nothing by the spectacle of those people who have so much. You will say, "Well, they do not see them." They do see them! It's brought to them by movies and by magazines and so forth, and they have constantly before their eyes the image of people who can have anything they want, apparently, without any trouble. So this is a tremendous problem.

We have to be humble, realistic. I would say that it's probably true to say that we could be much more poor than we are. Here is an enormous problem. I hate to talk to the novices about poverty because as soon as you do you run slap up into all kinds of contradictions. So I think one of the basic things we have to do, we have to accept these contradictions and try to do something about it without getting pig-headed about it. There is no point in getting stubborn about it. There is no point in deciding to lay down the law in poverty to your Superior and so forth. You can't do that. But, nevertheless, there is a problem and we run into constant contradictions.

For example, let me examine my own conscience in your presence (not all of it, I assure you!). But there's just this matter of poverty. I've got a room back there that is absolutely cluttered with all kinds of books and magazines and all sorts of things. Once a month I make an effort to clean things out. And they go out one window, and they come in the door. Somebody has called this the age of waste paper. Well, this is certainly the age when everything accumulates. And ... well, I suppose it would be possible to throw all those books out of there completely—and here are the kinds of alternatives you are faced with. Should I give them to the monastic library? But I can't put most of those books in the monastic library because they are forbidden books. And I have to read forbidden books. I don't have to read all forbidden books; I don't have to read all the forbidden books which are sent me, but I have to read some forbidden books. So I can't put them in the library, and I can't send them over here to you as a present. And...

Does that mean we have to stop?
*It's the supper bell, Father.*
Well, all right! Keep the vows and God bless you!
May the blessing of God Almighty, the Father, the Son and Holy Ghost descend upon you and remain forever. Amen.
Pray for me!

## Endnotes

1. Victor A. Kramer, ed., *Turning Toward the World: The Journals of Thomas Merton* Volume Four 1960-1963 (San Francisco: Harper San Francisco, 1997), 193-194.

2. See Thomas Merton, *Seeking Paradise: The Spirit of the Shakers* (Paul M. Pearson, ed.)(Maryknoll, NY: Orbis Books, 2003).

3. William B. Shannon, ed., *Thomas Merton Witness to Freedom: Letters in Times of Crisis* (New York: Farrar, Straus, Giroux, 1994), 53.

4. Ascension is the commemoration of Christ's return to heaven after the resurrection. See Acts of the Apostles, chapter 1.

5. Merton here paraphrases Romans 10:6-8 which includes the quotation about the Word found in Deuteronomy 30:14.

6. See Merton's journal entry for January 12, 1962, in *Turning Toward the World*, 194.

7. It is worth remembering that Merton is saying these things just as he is about to be silenced, told, under obedience, not to write any more on issues of war and peace.

8. Mary and Martha appear in Luke 10:38-42. They are traditional representatives of the contemplative life (Mary) and the active life (Martha).

9. Julian of Norwich (ca. 1342-1416) was an English woman who received 16 "showings" of divine love in 1373. She became an anchoress in Norwich, England. She understood Christ and Divine Providence to protect all people from ultimate harm. Merton had been reading Julian at the end of 1961. There is a long entry on her thought in his journal "December 27, 1961. St. John." (*Turning Toward the World*, 189-190.) There Merton calls Julian "one of my best friends" and "a true theologian." (p. 189). And see Merton's "The English Mystics" in *Mystics and Zen Masters* (New York: Farrar, Straus, Giroux, 1967).

10. John Henry Newman (1801-1890), famous defender of orthodox Christianity, was a well-known Anglican and one of the leaders of the Oxford Movement. He became a Roman Catholic in 1845 and a Cardinal in 1879.

11. Luke 17:11-19.

12. Mark 5:24-34.

# Two Letters of May 29, 1962

In order to give a broader sense of Merton's deep engagement with Loretto, these two letters, one of which appeared in edited form in *Witness to Freedom*, are, through the kind permission of the original publisher, included in their entirety here.[1] The first of the two, which was not reproduced in that collection, is important because it gives an indication of Merton's frame of mind after he was "silenced" from writing on peace. The book referred to in the note to Mother Luke is *Peace in the Post-Christian Era*, which was finally published in 2004.[2] Merton's friendship with and confidence in Luke Tobin is evidenced by his simple request here for her prayers. He "let her in" on one of the most stressful experiences in his monastic writing career.

The longer of the two letters is indicative of Merton's concern, in particular, for the novices at Loretto with whom he had already spoken on January 10, 1962 (see previous section), but, more generally, for religious formation. He had had significant opportunity to think about the matter as he had undertaken the responsibilities of both Master of Scholastics and Master of Novices at Gethsemani. It is touching that he refers to the young Loretto Sisters as "neighbors and friends" on earth and in heaven. The gentle reference to "trial" as "necessary" is especially poignant in view of his own circumstances.

These two letters are but one example of the lively correspondence between Loretto and Gethsemani, especially between Merton and Sr. Luke Tobin. Merton wrote a long letter to Sr. Helen Jean Seidel, SL, then Mistress of Novices, on October 9, 1961, clarifying what he had previously said to her novices on "mental prayer." Excerpts of that letter appear in *The School of Charity*,[3] the collection of Merton's letters on matters related to religious life and spiritual direction. The volume includes portions of nine letters Merton wrote to Luke between 1964 and 1968. (She is also mentioned in letters to Fr. Illtud Evans, Sr. Elaine M. Bane and Sr. N. in this volume and to Rosemary Radford Ruether in *The Hidden Ground of Love*.[4]) The subjects of the published letters include Luke's position as official auditor at Vatican II and especially the important Schema 13 (letter of July 7, 1965), Merton's transition to his hermitage and plans for the meetings with superiors of contemplative women's communities, the transcripts of which are published in *The Springs of Contemplation*.[5] Merton wrote to Sr. Luke on May 1, 1968, the day he left for California and Asia, another indication of the importance of that friendship.

Scholars and friends of Loretto may be interested to know that there are in the Thomas Merton Center at Bellarmine University two folders of correspondence between Luke Tobin and Thomas Merton that span the years from 1960 to 1968.[6] The first folder covers the years 1960 to 1964 and contains 13 letters from Merton to Luke and 2 letters and 4 post cards from Luke to Merton. Beyond what has been published, the material is not substantive, but "chatty," and reflective of the biographies and growing friendship of the two correspondents. The second folder covers the years 1965-1968 and contains 9 letters from Merton to Luke and 7 letters and 6 postcards from Luke to Merton (whom, by now, she calls "Tom"). The substantive material here concerns the Council and plans for the meeting of contemplative prioresses. The earlier bits of correspondence are more formal, but the exchange becomes freer as the friendship between Luke and Merton grows. The notes, letters and cards give many details of the visits between the two friends and are thus further evidence of the connection between Loretto and Gethsemani.[7]

## Endnotes

1. William H. Shannon, ed., *Thomas Merton, Witness to Freedom: Letters in Times of Crisis* (New York: Farrar, Straus, Giroux, 1994), 53-54.

2. Patricia A. Burton, ed., *Thomas Merton: Peace in the Post-Christian Era* (Maryknoll, NY: Orbis Books, 2004).

3. Br. Patrick Hart, ed., *Thomas Merton, The School of Charity: Letters on Religious Renewal and Spiritual Direction* (New York: Harcourt, Brace, Jovanovich, 1993), 140-141.

4. *School of Charity,* 252-53, 339-40, 355-56 and William H. Shannon, ed., *Thomas Merton, The Hidden Ground of Love: Letters on Religious Experience and Social Concerns* (New York: Farrar, Straus, Giroux, 1985), 499-500.

5. Jane Marie Richardson, SL, ed., *The Springs of Contemplation* (New York: Farrar, Straus, Giroux, 1992).

6. I am grateful to Dr. Paul Pearson, Curator of the Merton Collection at Bellarmine University, for permission to view these folders.

7. The official biography of Thomas Merton by Michael Mott, *The Seven Mountains of Thomas Merton* (Boston: Houghton, Mifflin, Co., 1984) provides a great deal of detailed information on the relationship between Sr. Luke and Fr. Louis/Thomas Merton. (See, for example, pages 410-411, 421-422, 447, 495 and the notes on those passages.) Mott rightly focuses on the importance of Merton's friendship with Sr. Luke. See also, Bonnie Thurston, "'I Never Had a Sister': Merton's Friendships with Women," *The Merton Seasonal* 17/1 (1992) and "'The Best Retreat I Ever Made': Merton and the Contemplative Prioresses," *The Merton Annual* 14 (2001) and Rose Annette Liddell, SL, "A Creative Exchange: The Mary Luke Tobin-Thomas Merton Friendship," *The Merton Seasonal* 32.2 (Summer 2007), 36-40.

Abbey of Gethsemani
Trappist, Kentucky

May 29, 1962

Dear Mother Luke:

A quick note to you with this little letter I wrote to the vow class. I shall be there in spirit on Thursday. Ascension Day is the anniversary of my ordination—not the exact date, that was May 26. It is a beautiful feast, my favorite I think. I forget if they made vows on ascension last year. Probably not.

I haven't seen Dan[1] and don't know where he is these days.

Do say some special prayers for me. Having a hard time with the work. The higher superiors have decided I must write no more on peace, which is all right. But I just finished that book about it I was writing.[2] It cannot be published. So I have to make the sacrifice instead, and no doubt that will be more fruitful. Other publishing affairs are in a tangle too, so I can use the help of the Holy Spirit even more than usual.

With very best wishes and blessings to all at Loretto,

Cordially yours in Christ Jesus,

[signed] Fr. M. Louis

The following letter is to the profession class of May 31, 1962. This class would have been received into the congregation on May 31, 1960. They would have attended Merton's "talks to the novices." This vow letter appears in *Witness to Freedom: Letters in Times of Crisis* (ed. Shannon), with a headnote paraphrasing Merton's letter (above) to Luke. The vow letter in the book has an error in the headnote, saying the novices are making FINAL vows. Also, the last paragraph in the vow letter, starting "I shall remember…," is omitted in the book.

Abbey of Gethsemani<br>Trappist, Kentucky

May 29, 1962
My Dear Sisters:

The day has come for you to give yourselves completely to Christ Our Lord. You will never appreciate, in this life, what it means to surrender yourself totally to Him. This must, from now on, be part of the mystery of faith in which you live. You will not *know* that you belong to Him; you must *believe* it. And this will require more faith than you have had up to this time. But He will give you the faith to believe it.

In the beginning, perhaps, this faith will not be too difficult. Later on, under trial, it may become hard at times. A faith that is not tested is not worth much. Your faith must grow always, without ceasing. That is why trial is necessary.

The faith of a first communicant is not enough for a postulant in religion. The faith of a postulant is not enough for a novice. The faith of a novice is not enough for a professed, and the faith of a newly professed is not enough for one who has been years in religion.

Sometimes we think that the purity of our faith is all in the past and that what we have to do is "recover" the fervor of our first communion, or of our days in the novitiate. On the contrary, we must go forward, not back. And going forward may at times be grim, because later on, when we go forward, we realize that we are getting to the end. However, at that time whatever was valuable in the beginning will be brought back to us in a new form by the Holy Spirit. It is not for us to be anxious about arranging our lives, even our spiritual lives.

If we belong to Christ, we must also believe that He belongs to us. And that is much more important. That is why we do not have to run our lives, for He is our life. We must not imagine that we can dictate to Him. Our gift of ourselves to Him is a surrender in joy, so that we henceforth allow Him to have His way with us.

Wherever you may go from here, remember me and pray for me. I will also remember you and keep you in my Masses and prayers. For since Our Lord has made us neighbors and friends on earth, I presume He wants us to be neighbors and friends in heaven also. But first we must accomplish our assigned tasks on this earth, whatever they may be. Let us keep praying for one another that we may do this well, and with confidence and joy, without anxiety, trusting in Him to whom we belong.

I shall remember you in a very special way at Mass this Thursday, and if it turns out that I have a Mass intention to dispose of, I shall offer it for you, together with my own novices. I do not yet know if I will be able to do this.

Meanwhile, God bless you.

Very cordially yours in Christ.

Father Louis Merton

## Endnotes

1. Dan Walsh, a friend of Merton's, taught at Loretto's junior college beginning in October 1960. He was still there in April 1962 and was ordained in 1967.

2. The reference is to *Peace in the Post-Christian Era* which was finally published in 2004 by Orbis Books. Patricia A. Burton edited the work, and Merton's friend Jim Forest provided a foreword.

# Talk of Father Louis to Novices and Postulants
## May 15, 1963

### Introductory Note

In early May 1963, Merton was struggling with the violence of police response to civil rights demonstrators in Alabama and with the categorical refusal from the Abbot General for permission to publish the manuscript *Peace in the Post-Christian Era* (which, in fact, was not published until 2004). On May 15, 1963, he wrote to John Harris, a schoolteacher in England who had been introduced to him by Boris Pasternak.[1] The subject of the fragment of the letter that appears in *The Hidden Ground of Love* is the publication of their letters, which Merton does not favor. Merton says Harris may quote his letters in an article provided he omits "My rather more lurid references to the Roman Curia and their hopeless delays, myopia, stupidity and so on."[2] Merton promises Harris some material he has written on peace, Fénelon[3] and Zen.

There is no journal entry for May 15. The entry for May 11 is comprised largely of notes on Louis Massignon's *Parole Donnée*.[4] The next entry, May 20, reflects Merton's irritation with the assumption he will give conferences to monks visiting Gethsemani, although he is not allowed to visit other monasteries where he has been invited to speak. He notes "...this upsets me so that I cannot sleep" and "Everyone can come and see me in my cage...."[5] On May 21 he admits his previous entry was "sick,"[6] and is much more circumspect.

The transcript of this talk provided an interesting editorial problem. There were four single-spaced pages on prayer stapled together, then two more single-spaced pages, also stapled. The first set of pages closes with a question in caps followed by an answer. The second set of pages follows the same format. All the pages are apparently from the same typewriter. Pages 1-4 and the set of two pages had each been stapled, the staples removed and then re-stapled. It is my considered opinion that all this material belongs to the same talk, and I have presented it as such below but with an extra white space after page four of the first document and before page one of the second.

### Merton's Talk

In prayer don't measure everything by your expectations, and when you're starting out (I don't know, maybe the postulants are all still on cloud nine) in prayer, in everything else, you've got to be very realistic in the spiritual life—all through—but especially in prayer. Don't be misled by books on prayer. There are an awfully lot of misleading ideas we can get about prayer which create the sort of impression that when you appear before God in prayer tremendous things are expected of you, all sorts of things that you're supposed to be able to do, and you're supposed to please Him by fantastic exploits, like being not distracted, that sort of thing. It's impossible not to be distracted.

And, in that connection, I think I could give you one general principle that goes for the whole life of man: watch out for impractical ideals. Because the impractical ideal is the kind that you work out in your head first, *a priori*, as the philosophers say. You work it out before, and then you apply it to reality, and you try to force reality to fit the ideal. You say reality has to be this way because this is the way it says in the book. And then when reality doesn't fit the ideal, you start fighting reality.

Don't let your prayer be a fight against reality. And the first reality you've got is yourself, and that's where prayer begins. It begins with you, and you don't have to go from you to God, because God is in you. All you've got to do is to stay where you are. You don't have to get out of this base earthly being which you are and climb Jacob's ladder and get way up in the heavens where God is, because if you do that, you'll never pray. You couldn't pray.

You have to start where you are and stay with it, because He is in you as you are, and He doesn't expect you to be any other than you are, except that there is a change that He is going to make in your life. But you have to learn how to get together with Him in your life so that He can make this change.

There are two things that you have to look out for, two extremes: on the one hand, an impractical idealism and on the other hand, a kind of passive realism. The impractical idealism is the kind that says, you know, as I said a moment ago... "I've worked it out beforehand and that's the way it's got to be." On the other hand, the wrong kind of realism says, "Well, this is the way it is. What can you do?" and just does nothing.

Both these views are basically pagan, and both are basically static; that is to say, they never get anywhere. In between, there is another view, which is the Christian view, which is: in the reality which I have and am now, there is a possibility for growth which God has put there. There's a seed[7] that He's planted there, and He's going to make grow in His own way, and what I have to provide is the love and the assent and the submission that's going to permit this to grow. I have to let this grow. I have to let the changes take place in my life that God wants to have take place in my life. If you think a little bit about that, you'll see that all the virtues that you can possibly think of are included in that—in letting God develop your life and change your life the way He wants.

It's going to take a lot of faith, a lot of hope, and you've got to love His will to let Him do this in you. The thing that makes this hard is precisely that we are what we are—because that's the last thing in the world that we want to accept—to be just what we are. If only we could be different. "If only I could be Sister so and so. If I could be even this one or that one." I've got to be me, and I'm not going to be anyone else but me, except that in being myself I can be Christ. And this we have to understand.

Now, to see that, we have to realize that we have a sort of a false self[8] which—this is the source of the conflict in us—is the self that we build out of everyday experience and out of our disappointments, and our reactions to disappointments. As we go through life we get hit, and we get kicked and so forth. We get stepped on. And each time we react to that, we make ourselves a sort of reacting being. We develop habits of self-defense, protecting ourselves and justifying ourselves, and then after we've been at this for a number of years, we've got an alibi for everything. And this is a waste of time. We've put in a great deal of useless effort on this—all this mental activity building up the self which is justified.

Now this has a great deal to do with what St. Paul says about "we are justified by faith."[9] In a certain sense, we are justified by faith because it takes faith to get rid of all this. He's really making a contrast between the man who feels himself justified by the testimony of his conscience which believes in God. If my conscience says "yes" to Christ, that's enough. He will take care of it—He will justify me. It is Christ who will justify me. That's the meaning of the Cross. The meaning of our Lord on the Cross is that we don't have to justify ourselves because He has justified us on the Cross. We don't have to be right in this external self. We are right in Him if we follow His will; then what we do is right because that's what He wants. We may not understand it, perhaps, but it doesn't matter.

Well, prayer is work, but it's a very special kind of delicate work in which we have to let Our Lord do what He wants, and the dead spots in prayer are very important. The fact that you may not be able to pray for days on end doesn't matter; it may be worthwhile. It's just like the winter in the life of a plant.[10] The plants aren't wasting time in the winter; they're not losing anything. Winter is very important for the plant, and these periods of stillness and incapacity may be, actually, the best things in your life of prayer. You don't know.

If you go into prayer with the idea that when you're distracted and bored and sleepy, that you're purely and simply losing time, you're making a mistake, but if you just simply accept it in the wrong way you're making a mistake, too. What you have to do is realize that in this time of boredom and distraction and weariness, Our Lord is working, and you've got to let Him work, and you've got to want Him, if necessary, to lead you to suffering in your prayer. If He does, all right. And the suffering is in the dimension of being bored, being dry and feeling useless, feeling that you're not getting any place. One of the best things in your life is to feel that you're not getting any place because that's when Our Lord really can do something with you if you let Him. You don't *want* to get any place. You want to go where He leads you—not to follow any project of your own and come out with something that *you* want.

So, all through your life of prayer, it's that kind of thing. When you can work, when you can do something, when you can make acts, fine. Don't feel guilty about that. The great thing is not to lay down the law to Our Lord. Let Him do what He wants. If He wants you to be consoled, thank Him; if He wants you to be dry, thank Him. What this boils down to is great respect for life and great respect for the way life works ... organic and spontaneous living being.

This is the most important thing in our time, and this, because it's so important, is the thing that Religious have to provide in our time and this, believe me, is the thing that Sisters have to provide. Your vocation is of tremendous importance. You are tremendously important because you're going to be dealing with children. The child is going to come to you with marvelous natural qualities that are yet unspoiled—or perhaps maybe they get spoiled quickly now, but still, when they come to you, there will be these qualities, this spontaneity and love and life and things like that, and you've got to be very careful that you don't step on this, block it and frustrate it, knock it down and so forth.

It takes a great deal of humility and guidance from the Holy Spirit to respect the life that's in these children. There's always a temptation to prefer what's in the book to what the kid's doing. Without just letting him do anything he wants, you should respect the fact that this life in the child is something that's put there by God and acts according to God. Nature is from God. Nature isn't a bad thing. Nature is a good thing, but it mustn't just run wild. So that we have to learn that God may be speaking even in the nature of children, even in our own nature, our own feeling or something like that may have something from God.

A respect for life is going to help you most in prayer, because prayer is a living thing. What does Our Lord compare it to (the best place to find out about prayer is in the Gospel)? Our Lord says it's a spring of living water.[11] St. Ignatius of Antioch[12] says that the Holy Spirit in our heart is like a spring of running water, welling up in our heart saying, "Come to the Father." What do you want better than that? You've got the whole theology of prayer in that. So what we are doing in prayer is we are being led by the Spirit of life through the Son to the Father.

Prayer is the Trinitarian life of God in us. It's dynamic in this way. It is a movement. When you're dry and helpless, that movement is still taking place; if you can handle that, you can go along with it, especially at Communion. That's what the mystery of the Eucharist is, among other things, not only in the individual but in the whole community. This movement of love is taking place in the Father and the Son and the Holy Spirit. So, keep your faith in life, not only in natural life, but above all in this divine life.

### What are the fruits of prayer in daily life?

I think a person who is really living a life of prayer should in his daily life be very simple and relaxed and natural in a good sense. Don't be afraid to look for fruits of prayer even on a very simple natural level. Here's the thing: if your prayer is making you impatient and angry and critical and all those things, watch it a little bit. Because that means it isn't living enough, your will is in there trying to twist the Holy Ghost's arm, so to speak. There's a little force in there.

This doesn't mean that the prayer is bad. It means that one's will is too active. It means that we're pushing. These are little signs, like impatience. Impatience is a most important thing in the spiritual life. It's an indicator. It's like something that hurts on your foot, like a nail in your shoe. When you begin to feel your foot hurting in a certain spot, you realize there's a nail sticking into your foot there, and so you get the nail out. Well, that's what impatience is like. We're impatient when we've got a nail sticking in us somewhere, usually from our own will, and if we can do something about it, fine; if we can't well—sometimes you just have to stay with that nail for a long time.

But the real fruits of prayer in everyday life are along the line of humility, simplicity, and a kind of acceptance—the ability to accept ourselves and a willing ability to accept our Sisters. You can't reject anybody. That's a very important fruit of prayer. Of course, we can come from prayer still feeling antipathy to people. That doesn't matter, but we can have the willingness not to reject anybody. That's the Gospel, you see. Our Lord says that when you go to pray you shouldn't have any animosity toward anybody; you should forgive everybody.[13]

It is a very important thing to distinguish between this false self that I was talking about—the kind that we build up with our own will, the self-justifying self; that's not Christ; that's what's opposed to Him. And of course that's what has to die. When I say we must be ourselves, I mean die to self. You've got to die to self to be yourself. That's the mystery of all this. It's easy to apply this purely on a natural level, purely natural spontaneity and so forth. That doesn't work—then people start saying, "these rules are crazy," and all that, but of course these things are supposed to put to death the external self.

All this is to be understood on the basis of a total acceptance of your duties of state, your religious duties, your religious rules, those things. This is absolutely understood. You can't throw them over and then say "I'm just being myself now." There's where you get into all kinds of trouble because this is a non-acceptance; it's rejection—and the basic thing is you can't accept and reject at the same time. If our Lord is giving you your rule of life, your job and the people you have to associate with, you can't reject that and then say that you're united with Him. You have to accept those things, you see. So then, if you are accepting them and really praying, our Lord does live in you; but that's at the price of constant death.[14]

In prayer, how can you tell when it's the false self that is acting in prayer or your true self, when it seems that the false self is so much a part of you that you probably don't even know when it's taking place?

It's hard to tell until you get blocked, but as soon as you run into obstacles you can tell because then you get rattled; you get upset; you get scared. You should learn to know when there's an inordinate amount of self-defense and justification going on. It's justification which is a kind of good lead on that, I think. When you feel that there's a tremendous amount of activity going on inside to justify what you just did, watch it. Not that it's necessarily bad. It does mean, you see—if I'm defending something, it means that something's threatened, but my true self, strictly speaking, can't be threatened. Only this false self can be threatened in me. The true self is in Christ; you can't touch it. It can be threatened in the sense that my false self does threaten it, but you see, if I'm defending myself, well, maybe there are times when a person should, but then you have a different attitude. You have to kind of learn to distinguish a little bit. Sometimes you do have to put forth your viewpoint, but there are signs. There should be some indication that it's really God's will to do that, and that you should feel peaceful in doing it, and you accept the results (and if it's not accepted, well, you've thought of that, and so forth). But these moments when we're sort of grumbling and growling, "I'll tell her that she's not as smart as she thinks she is," and that kind of thing.

The less introspection, the better; we don't have to see what's going on in ourselves. We shouldn't look at ourselves. I don't know what you have for examination of conscience, but what I tell the novices over there for examination of conscience is to make a visit to the Blessed Sacrament and not think about themselves but simply open their heart to Him and let the light of God shine in their heart, and if there's anything in the way, they'll see it, and if there isn't anything in the way, they won't have to worry. You know if we can get out of ourselves and think of the things that are going on in the world and think of the issues that are so important in the world, we're not really distracted. The trouble is that some people are taught to regard those things as distractions. They're not. We should have compunction today for collective crime, because there's where compunction is called for. We're not called upon to have compunction because we were a little impatient or a little lazy or something like that. We're called upon to have compunction because of the H-bomb, etc. For this we should have deep compunction, for the business that's going on in the South, and for the whole peace issue. I really think that in our life of prayer, as far as I'm concerned, the question of distractions is gone when you get down to these big issues. You haven't got time to be distracted, because you realize that we're living in the age of the whole concentration camp thing, and all these atomic wars, and so forth.

You can see behind these happenings, what kind of a force was pushing the people, and that they didn't know what was happening, and why didn't they know? Why does the world go on like this with people not knowing—it's because it has lost the sense of God and because religious people have lost the sense of God. Our life of prayer is in the light of this sort of thing. We've got to be people who belong to God and who reflect His truth in their life, whose life is simply filled with the light of His truth, who suffer with Him when His truth is denied.

So, I think that we should get away from the old books on prayer of the comfortable age when all people were worried about were their little imperfections, and they saw no further than their own individualistic growth of piety. If we can get away from that and see all these things in the light of a world in which God has placed light, life, love, and so forth...these things should grow in the world instead of being denied and repressed and so on and destroyed. Then we realize what the life of prayer really is.

The original word for compunction means something that pierces your heart. If your heart has compunction, it means that it's pierced by something. I think compunction begins when we look at these things, and our heart is pierced with sorrow at the fact that truth is derided and denied.

The basic example of compunction is looking at Christ on the Cross and realizing that this is Truth, this is He who loves us and has given everything for us, and we have caused this. This is compunction. You know, we all feel this at times. The Cross is the archetype of compunction, and this is the way prayer begins—with this kind of realization. Of course, it's a gift. It's not something that we can "just have." You can't have it by pressing a button. It has to be given by God, and the recognition that it's a gift is part of compunction, sort of a recognition that God has deigned to give me the light to see. He's had pity on me enough to see what is happening to the truth and all this is part of it, and this is a real grace.

Look at the Cross.[15] Everything centers on the Cross of our Lord, you see, and when you realize the meaning of the Cross, that's the beginner's lesson for everybody, really. There's a kind of a delightful compunction in the Gospel narrative of the Nativity, for example, the Christmas Gospel. Even though it's midrash and all that. Father Barnabas Mary gave us a very good talk on the literary forms of the Nativity narratives in the Gospel, and it makes it much more striking than the more conservative view. The conservative view is afraid of this type of thing, but actually, it gives it more power; midrash is all right.[16]

Comments on recollection

You have to see recollection in terms of this unity business. If recollection is a matter of excluding anything, it's not going to work well. I used to try to make my thanksgiving by shutting out everything, and it was nice and very beautiful, and of course it was much earlier. There used to be a man that lived down the back road, and I remember that the best part of my novitiate thanksgiving was this man going to work at the distillery. Every morning as he went down the back road, he whistled the same sort of tune, one of his own tunes, and you'd hear him coming. He always came at the same time, and for some reason or another, that was a wonderful thing in that thanksgiving. Here was the world, see. Here was this lonely man on the back road, and it meant a great deal. I never thought about it, but it stuck with me. Well, now, we bought out his property. He's not there anymore. He's farther down. He's nearer the distillery, so he's happier and we're happy. But now all the novices, and sometimes their novice master,[17] sleep during their thanksgiving. There's no reason to sleep up there at all because the place is full of birds. And if you simply listen to every one of the birds individually, which is heresy according to the spiritual books, for it's a deliberate distraction. Actually, it's a wonderful thanksgiving, because who made those birds, and who put them there, and who is making them sing, and who is the Source of their life? It is

He Who is in my heart and is the source of my life, and I'm one with all these things. And, we're all one in His love. And all the birds and all the people and everything, the whole world, is there. So, what I mean to say by that is that if I try to be recollected by excluding those birds, I'd be ruining my thanksgiving. Of course, I'm not deliberately thinking about birds all the time, but they're there, and it's a great help to thank Him.

## Endnotes

1. Soviet Russian poet, novelist and translator (1890-1960), perhaps best known in America for his novel *Dr. Zhivago* which was made into a movie.

2. William H. Shannon, ed., *Thomas Merton, The Hidden Ground of Love: Letters* (New York: Farrar, Straus, Giroux, 1985), 399.

3. François Fénelon (1651-1715), Catholic priest, educator and writer was interested in interior prayer and the spiritual life. Although he had difficulties with the magisterium, his work was influential in Europe and England in the eighteenth century. "Reflections on the Character and Genius of Fénelon," Introduction to *Fénelon: Letters of Love and Counsel*, trans. John McEwan (New York: Harcourt, Brace & World, 1964), 9-30.

4. Massignon, a French Roman Catholic, wrote extensively on Islam, especially Sufism. His greatest work is probably *The Passion of al-Hallaj*. Merton read his work in French and corresponded with him. Thomas Merton, *Witness to Freedom: Letters in Times of Crisis*, ed. William H. Shannon (New York: Farrar, Straus, Giroux, 1994), 275-81

5. Victor A. Kramer, ed., *Turning Toward the World: The Journals of Thomas Merton* Volume Four 1960-1963 (San Francisco: Harper San Francisco, 1997), 320.

6. Kramer, 321.

7. Merton may have in mind here the Parable of the Seed in Mark 4. He had recently revised *Seeds of Contemplation* for republication as *New Seeds of Contemplation*. Several ideas that appear in this talk are dealt with in more detail in that volume.

8. For a fuller discussion of the true and false selves see *New Seeds of Contemplation* (New York: New Directions, 1961), chapters 5-8.

9. Galatians 2:15-16.

10. See Merton's poem "Love Winter When the Plant Says Nothing" published in the 1963 collection *Emblems of a Season of Fury*. The poem is also in *The Collected Poems of Thomas Merton* (New York: New Directions, 1977), 353.

11. See John 4:7-15 and 7:38.

12. Third bishop of Antioch in Syria (c.35-c.107), author of early Christian epistles, who was martyred in Rome in the early second century.

13. Matthew 5:23-24 and 6:14-16.

14. This is the point at which the first four stapled pages end. The following material was separate and stapled together. See introduction to this talk.

15. Again this is a particularly powerful suggestion to the Sisters of Loretto at the Foot of the Cross.

16. Merton is alluding to the use of historical-critical methodologies in the interpretation of scripture. John Collins, "A Passionist Friendship: Barnabas Ahern and Thomas Merton," *The Merton Seasonal* 34.2 (Summer 2009), 17-29.

17. Merton! A description of the event appears in Jonathan Montaldo, ed., *Entering the Silence: The Journals of Thomas Merton* Volume Two 1941-1952 (San Francisco: Harper San Francisco, 1996), 481.

# Comments on the Vows

## Introductory Notes

The transcript of these comments on the vows has no indication of when they were given so no definite context can be provided. This transcript seems to be typed on the same machine and in the same style as the talk of May 15, 1963.

On November 1, 1964, Merton wrote to Sister Luke and mentioned copies of his talk he was sending to her. He reports the talk went well enough and that there was little discussion. He is sending her the talk and a copy of a longer version ("Identity Crisis and Monastic Vocation").[1] As the subject of the following comments is monastic vows they *might* be the document in question, but this is pure speculation on my part.

## Merton's Talk

In profession, you have certain necessary elements. Profession implies three things, only one of which is the public pronunciation of vows. There are two other elements that are necessary in profession. One is the dedication of your life to the following of Christ, and the other is incorporation in a religious community. These three things make up profession. We usually think of profession simply as making vows. The making of vows is the least important part of it. Much more important are these other two elements. First of all is the question of leaving all to follow Christ. That is the meaning of your profession. When you are making profession, that's what you're doing. You are leaving all. You are leaving the world and you are taking up your religious life as a Cross to follow Christ. And then, incorporation in the community is most important. You can't make religious profession unless you're incorporated in a community.

The most beautiful thing in our monastic ceremony happens after the monk has pronounced his solemn vows. The first thing he does is to sign a little schedule of profession in which he wrote out the vows; then he takes the schedule of profession and lays it on the altar and kisses the altar. After this, he comes down from the altar and goes all round the community kneeling at the feet of each one; each one embraces him. While this is going on, the whole community is singing the *Miserere*.[2] There you've got the idea of second Baptism. The beautiful thing about it is that this incorporation into the community is not a juridical act only; it's a human act in which the person is incorporated into the love of the Community. The Community means love. The Community just doesn't mean a number of units in the same place. Where there is no love, there is no community. The fact of being together in the same physical environment doesn't constitute a community. When a person is accepted in a community, then what happens is that by love, by the combined love of the reception in the community and the abandoning of his whole life to follow Christ, there is the washing away of all his sins. This second Baptism is now to be seen in the light of this act of charity which runs through the whole Community.

Your vows take place immediately after Communion. This is simply acting out on a more visible level the mystery of the Eucharist. It comes to the same thing. Your profession is the same, because what is the Eucharist if not this going around and embracing everybody? We have the kiss of peace before Communion. Everybody who is going to Communion embraces everybody else—it goes down the line, which is I think a very fine thing. I guess Sisters couldn't do that, maybe your veils would get in the way. But this brings home the real meaning of Communion, and again it gets down to the realities of life. Because, I mean, you may fight with your Sisters, you know—I'm not advising you to, but you can't help it sometimes and this doesn't matter really. I mean, the little fighting once in a while doesn't really interfere with sincere love. Don't be disturbed by those things. There can be a great warmth and spontaneity of love even where there's friction. It doesn't matter, and I think that the attitude of seeing things as not mattering too much is very, very helpful.

About Poverty. Well, there are a lot of things to be said about that. In the Old Testament, the poor are very important people. God put the poor in Israel for a very special reason. They were there as a kind of trust that Israel was supposed to look after. There had to be poor people in Israel. They were there, and Israel had to look after them and take care of them, and as long as Israel was faithful to Yahweh, the poor were looked after and taken care of. And when Yahwehism declined and when you got the king and the temple and the state, and Israel became secularized, then there was the situation which the prophets keep inveighing against. And Amos said, "The poor man is sold for a pair of shoes,"[3] and the prophets are all the time rising up against this sacrilege of the poor being ignored. Because there's more to it than just simply a human question; God's honor is involved. When the poor are ignored, and His law is ignored, and His will is ignored so that it reflects on us, we become poor to protest, among other things, against the fact that the poor are looked down on. Now this is where it really begins to pinch, because are we that poor? But we've got to realize the real meaning of religious poverty is that we have freely chosen a state which the secular world despises and regards as unfortunate and regards as evil, and regards as something to avoid. And so we've embraced poverty for that reason, because God has placed a blessing on it, and we want to be with the poor people.

One of the great problems of religious life today is that we never feel the pinch. Oh, occasionally, when you want to get a permission and you can't get it. Poverty is not just a question of a Cadillac with permission. There has to be a pinch there somewhere. I think you may get it much more than we do. You may get out in some little part of the missions somewhere—of course if you go to South America, you'll see poverty. Just think how many people in this world don't have a bed to sleep on. They've never slept on anything but the floor; a dirt floor with rats running over them, that's what they're used to. How many people get more than one meal a day? Two-thirds of the world don't get more than just the bare necessities of life; so when we're embracing poverty, that's what we're embracing. We're embracing a state where we do have need, and we do feel necessity. So that if we do occasionally feel a bit of necessity in our life, we shouldn't worry about it too much. It's tremendous what we get. If you go to a hospital, you get the best of treatment, etc.

From the moment that you give yourself completely to God, from the moment that in your heart you are surrendering totally to God, there's no reason why it should not be a second Baptism. The only difference is that in profession there are signs that it's a second Baptism. The Church tells you so. The Church reassures you and says, "Yes, it is a second Baptism." When you're just entering, you've got no one telling you that—except I'll tell you that. The Church doesn't act it out. There's no sacramental symbolism that indicates this, whereas in profession, the Church formally accepts you, and it's pretty clear.

Again, it's this question of surrender. Marriage is mutual surrender. This is a giving. The parties to Matrimony hand themselves over to each other. They belong to each other. Well, now, this is much deeper. The thing about virginity, about consecrated virginity, is that paradoxically it is much more real than Matrimony. Virginity and consecrated virginity are not something kind of abstract, sort of a second best deal, but meritorious. On the contrary, some authors have even said that Matrimony is but a symbol and a sign of the reality which is in virginity. Now, there's a deep mystery in this. If Father Danielou[4] were here, he could give you something by the Greek Fathers. Every human being aspires to a unity in which there is neither male nor female.[5] A unity above the division. Well, all this would have to be spiritual, you see. In Matrimony, this unity would have to be achieved in married love, in which the two become one person.

Virginity restores the condition of man in Paradise. How? By elevating him to union with Christ in which there is no longer this division. See, in Christ there is no longer this division caused by the Fall. Love is what does this. This total surrender of love is what enables a person to lose his separateness. What we aspire to is this unity, and this is what your life as Bride of Christ is going to mean. It is going to mean a unity which contains all that is best in the spiritual aspect of marriage and much more. But for that, you truly have to be a bride of Christ. That means to say, a completely uncompromising renunciation of all that's not Christ in order to find Him in everybody. Because, you see, as a bride of Christ you've got to be a mother of the whole world. As a bride of Christ you can reject nobody. As a bride of Christ your heart is open to everybody; there's nobody to whom your heart is closed. And it is only by being united to Him that your heart can have that power. Naturally we don't have that power. It can't be done. This is something that we should really aspire to, and this is what it means to be a consecrated virgin, to have a heart that is open to everybody and that never says "no" to any legitimate need for love on the part of the Community. This has to be, of course, on a high spiritual level because you've got to belong to evcrybody, which means to say you can never narrow you heart down to one person. As soon as you become an object of love to some other subject, then you're "you" again, and you're back in your division. You're back in this little circle, and you're back where you started. And you can only break out of that by never being an exclusive object or an exclusive subject. You just can't be a subject loving somebody else as an exclusive object. As long as we're free from this exclusiveness, then our love is universal, and then Christ lives in us and loves in us. When we give Him our human heart, such as it is, He's got a real heart to love everybody with, and that's what we're supposed to do, is give Him our heart with which to love everybody.

## Endnotes

1. Br. Patrick Hart, ed., *Thomas Merton, The School of Charity: Letters on Religious Renewal and Spiritual Direction* (New York: Harcourt, Brace, Jovanovich, 1990), 250-251 and Thomas Merton, "The Identity Crisis," in *Contemplation in a World of Action* (Garden City, NY: Doubleday, 1971), 56-82.

2. Psalm 51 (50 in the Vulgate).

3. Amos 8:6.

4. (1905-1974) French Jesuit, patristic scholar, and important voice at the time of Vatican II.

5. See Galatians 3:28.

# Postscript

Thomas Merton, known to the community at Loretto by his "monastic name," Father Louis, spoke at Loretto of matters close to his own heart: the monastic life of prayer and peace and justice. Four themes seemed to me to emerge as central to what Merton wanted to say to his friends at Loretto.

The first theme is that of vocation, what it means to be called by God to religious life, indeed, to the life of the Christian in an uncertain and violent world. Merton speaks of this both in terms of call and of the traditional monastic vows of poverty, chastity and obedience. Intrinsically related to the matter of vocation is that of the life of God living itself *in* Christians, specifically in the sisters themselves. Merton speaks of God and Christ living in the sisters as their "true self," a theme which is central in the early chapters of *New Seeds of Contemplation* which he was revising in the early 1960s.

Third, expanding on traditional Pauline theology,[1] Merton reminded the sisters of the "power of weakness" and, consequently, of the importance of the cross. Especially this latter would have been helpful to and important theologically for young women who had joined the Congregation of the Sisters of Loretto at the Foot of the Cross as the community was called. Merton wrote in "Loretto and Gethsemani," "It is clear...that our vocation to love the truth is also a vocation to love the Cross. Our lives therefore are to be led purely and simply under a sign of contradiction."[2] It is, I think, what he spoke so eloquently of as the contradiction of strength in weakness, the strength and weakness of a love that leads to crucifixion and resurrection, death and life.

Finally, Merton regularly warned the sisters of the danger of trying to follow too closely devotional manuals, books on how to pray, spiritual "rules" of any sort. He was encouraging them to let their lives of prayer develop, grow from the seed God planted in them, in short, to evolve naturally. He was not suggesting they ignore their rule of life. On the contrary he speaks of the necessity of obedience. The real point, and the important one, is that Merton was reminding the sisters not to take themselves too seriously. He reminded them that, in the light of the massive evil which shadowed them, the "little problems" of religious life were just that, little problems. One often hears the refrain, "it doesn't matter too much," or words to that effect. Those who are called to address real suffering and evil in the world—and Merton is clear that the sisters' vocation involves just that—must in their own lives "lighten up." It is good advice to all of us.

Thomas Merton (and, indeed, Sister Mary Luke Tobin) saw life as a whole. He encouraged the nuns of Loretto to be unified people, integrated women. That, finally, was their "work."

> If the Lord of all took flesh and sanctified all nature, restoring it to the Father by his resurrection, we too have our work to do in extending the power of the resurrection to the whole world of our time by our prayer, our thought, our work and our whole life. Nothing so effectively prevents this as the division, the discontinuity of spiritual lives that place God and prayer in one compartment, work and apostolate in another, as if prayer and work were somehow opposed. The Cross is the sign of contradiction, but also and above all the sign of reconciliation. It reminds us of the contradictions within ourselves, and within our society, only in order to resolve them all in unity and in love of the Savior.[3]

Merton's 1962 essay, "Loretto and Gethsemani," which follows, was written to celebrate the 150th anniversary of Loretto's founding. It emphasizes the centrality of the Cross. The editors hope that sharing this essay and these notes from Merton's conferences in the early 1960s will help us all to "extend the power of the resurrection to the whole world."

Endnotes

1. For more on this see Bonnie Thurston, "'No longer I who live': Notes on Thomas Merton and St. Paul," *The Merton Seasonal* 34/1 (Spring 2009), 14-19.

2. Thomas Merton, "Loretto and Gethsemani," 8; this essay appears in this volume.

3. Ibid., 7.

# Loretto and Gethsemani

*By Thomas Merton*

In Commemoration of the 150th Anniversary of
the Founding of the Congregation of
The Sisters of Loretto at the Foot of the Cross

1812–1962

We are not only neighbors in a valley that is still lonely, but we are equally the children of exile and of revolution. Perhaps this is a good reason why we are both hidden in the same mystery of Our Lady's Sorrow and Solitude in the Lord's Passion. We cannot understand our vocation except in the light of that solitude and that love, in which we are as inextricably one as the bones of the founders of two Gethsemanis in one grave: the first Lorettine nuns who dedicated the place to Mary and the first Breton Trappists who took it over from them. All who were buried in back of the Dant house, the log cabin that was the first Gethsemani, are now together under the nameless concrete cross behind the Abbey Church. Their anonymity, their community in death, is eloquent: but probably most of us have ceased to notice it, or have never even been aware of it in the first place.

\* \* \*

Father Nerinckx was born in 1761, in Brabant—a region[1] which was perhaps more fertile in Cistercian saints than any other. He fled to America from the Revolutionary armies of France and from the constitutional oath which he could not take. He was appointed to Kentucky, where Father Badin was the only priest. He started west in 1805 with the first Trappist colony, Dom Urban Guillet's fugitives from Napoleonic France. But Father Nerinckx moved faster and reached Kentucky before them. He helped them get settled in Holy Cross and Casey Creek. He spent days and nights in their monastery when he was able. He wanted to become one of them. He had the same rigid, austere, uncompromising and generally unsmiling spirit. Like them he saw all things in black and white: it was simpler that way, though not always more revealing. He never managed to obtain permission to join the monks. If he had done so, he would presently have left Kentucky with them forever, and returned to France. Instead of that he built St. Stephen's and helped to establish a seminary there. On that same site the Loretto Motherhouse now stands.

Father Nerinckx founded one of the first completely American Congregations of Sisters. The nuns were Catholic pioneers who had come from

Maryland to Nelson County[2] and who started a school in an abandoned, broken-down log cabin in 1812. They refused to let Sisters be called from Europe to give shape to the new Institute. They knew what shape they wanted to give it. They knew how to grow and acquire the spirit willed by God, under the guidance of their Director. The rugged simplicity of Loretto still has a healthy, early American quality about it. One does not sense there too many of the rigid and deadening formalities which many other Congregations have brought from across the ocean.

* * *

It was five years after the Congregation of Loretto came into existence that the Dant family gave them a house on Pottinger's Creek, which had long been a mission station. In 1818 the nuns started a school there and called it Gethsemani. They operated this school for thirty years, and then a Trappist monk from France, a Father Paulinus, of the Abbey of Melleray, appeared in the county looking for land. It was once again a year of revolution, and the Trappists of Melleray, near Nantes, were threatened with expulsion. Father Paulinus agreed to buy this farm and at the end of 1848 a colony of monks took it over from the Sisters. They settled down to till the fields in silence. It is not recorded that they were very often aware of the existence of nearby Loretto. But I suppose that from the earliest days there have been occasionally seen, in the back of our Church, the black habits of the Lorettines. Pardon me, not seen. We like to believe that we never look.

Quietly, efficiently, the Lorettines began to spread out over the country, westward, and southward. Already before the end of the nineteenth century they had raised many of the ponderous brick academies fashionable at that time. The Trappists stayed in their valley. They were busy keeping body and soul together. They too had an academy. They even started a congregation of nuns of their own, which got away from them in a storm of juridical red tape and drifted to Indiana.[3] And after that the boys' school burned down and the Trappists went out of business as educators. Loretto continued to grow and to prosper. The Trappists continued to exist.

Until finally, at the end of the Second World War, Gethsemani stirred to life. Two Cistercian foundations went south. Two went west, one went north. No one has yet explained why, suddenly, so many Americans wanted to become Cistercians. Such things do not need to be explained. In any case, explanations are misleading. There are things about Gethsemani that cannot be put into any words whatever; still less can they be comprehensively published for the edification of multitudes.

There is something about Gethsemani that has nothing to communicate to multitudes: and I find it also at Loretto. It is a secret that reveals itself only partially even to those who live for a long time in our valley.

I suppose I will give scandal if I say it is a quiet mixture of wisdom and madness, a triumph of hope over despair. But we have both descended from ancestors who died accomplishing the impossible. Or rather from people who accepted as perfectly normal the incongruity and solitude which are the lot of the pioneer. Now we are safer than they, richer, more comfortable, better cared for, secure. But when I say there is madness in the old walls of our houses, I mean a wise madness that still, for all the public approval we have received from "the world," persists in a half-ironic suspicion that all is not well with the world, and that we cannot be altogether part of it. This I know is the thing I must not say. We are of course *engagés*. We are in the world of our time, no doubt about that. We are in it to save it. Yet we still have to save ourselves from it, for unless we have a foothold that is not of the world, we will go down with it, and drag no one to safety.

* * *

You are Daughters, not of the American, but of the French Revolution. Hence daughters not on Park Avenue but in this hot valley, and at the foot of the Cross. I think we have to remember that if we pray for the people on Park Avenue, no less than for those on Skid Row, we are not praying for Park Avenue or for Skid Row as such. We are not satisfied with the *status quo*, no matter how plush it may be for very many. The point of our striving is not that the world should be rich, but that it should be Christian. And in a time like ours, at least in this country, there is always the satanic temptation to identify holiness with prosperity. It has become an old habit of our rich nation to turn the beatitudes inside out and to assume that we must indeed be meek because we have inherited the land. Especially somebody else's land. In a word, we have reaped the harvest sown by the pioneers and it is enormous. Yet we have assumed that because they were courageous they had, perhaps, all the other virtues together with fortitude: and that because we are the richest people in the world we are also the most righteous.

* * *

It is true that our adversaries have the luxury of proclaiming themselves godless and they can dispense from asking themselves questions like these. We who are consecrated to Christ retain the dubious privilege of acting as a kind of conscience in a confused and increasingly conscienceless world of pragmatism and *laissez faire*. In this society of ours we must frankly admit a tragic intellectual and moral incoherence where the only universal principle is "whatever works is right." Then when things stop working, all is wrong. Our Christian ethic is not based on any such relativism. Our standards rise above the fluctuations and accidents of sociological change.

In Christ, God has revealed to us His will, His love and His truth; and we have accepted this revelation by freely choosing to be loyal to Christ and His Church in prosperity and adversity, war and peace, in freedom or in prison. This loyalty is the price and guarantee of the only true freedom—and it is on this ideal that the culture of the Christian west has been built. Now that the west has rejected this ideal, and forfeited its spiritual inheritance, the task of those consecrated to God in religion becomes increasingly difficult. The difficulty itself is, then, essential to our vocation. Only by accepting the fact that we are in some sense exiles at odds with materialism, commercialism and secularism can we begin to be fully faithful to Christ. We must sometimes be resolutely unfashionable, both in morals and in intelligence. This does not mean a cult of anachronism: on the contrary, it is a kind of dissent which is necessary for genuine growth. And Christian dissent is all the more essential as we enter what C. S. Lewis has called the *post-Christian* era.

Let us be persuaded that we can dissent without at the same time becoming fanatics, but that our first duty is to preserve the purity of our faith.

\* \* \*

There is nothing more positive, more creative than the faith by which the Creator of all dwells and acts in our hearts. And yet, as we know from our own past history, the ideal of "keeping the faith" can sometimes dwindle into something very negative, resentful and obtuse: a mere "no" to everything that we do not agree with. We can no longer afford to barricade ourselves in our Catholic environment and regard it as a little smug fortress of security in a world of pagans. Now most of all we are obliged by our faith and by our love of truth to commit ourselves humbly and completely not only to the message of Christ but also to all that is valid in human culture and civilization: for this, too, is His by right. Not only is it something that we must salvage for Him, but more, it is not unconnected with our own salvation. If the Lord of all took flesh and sanctified all nature, restoring it to the Father by His resurrection, we too have our work to do in extending the power of the resurrection to the whole world of our time by our prayer, our thought, our work and our whole life. Nothing so effectively prevents this as the division, the discontinuity of spiritual lives that place God and prayer in one compartment, work and apostolate in another, as if prayer and work were somehow opposed. The Cross is the sign of contradiction, but also and above all the sign of reconciliation. It reminds us of the contradictions within ourselves, and within our society, only in order to resolve them all in unity in love of the Savior. Unity is the sign of strength and spiritual health. This unity in Christ is the true secret of our Christian and religious vocations, whether our lives be active or contemplative.

False unity is the work of force. It is violently imposed on divided entities which stubbornly refuse to be one. True unity is the work of love. It is the free union of beings that spontaneously seek to be one in the truth, preserving and elevating their separate selves by self-transcendence. False unity strives to assert itself by the denial of obstacles. True unity admits the presence of obstacles, and of divisions, in order to overcome both by humility and sacrifice.

Here, in facing contradiction, we can hope for grace from God that will produce a unity and a peace "which the world cannot give."

* * *

It is clear, then, that our vocation to love the truth is also a vocation to love the Cross. Our lives therefore are to be led purely and simply under a sign of contradiction. This may sometimes create much anguish both for ourselves and for those who come in contact with us. But this anguish is our inheritance. It is our substitute for the solitude and insecurity of the pioneer. The Christian life is not an enclosed garden in which we can sit at ease, protected by the love of God: it is also, alas, a wilderness into which we can be led by the Spirit in order to be tempted by the devil.

Or, a Garden where, while Christ sweats Blood in an agony beyond our comprehension, we struggle to keep awake under the moonlit olive trees.

## Endnotes

1. Brabant is a region of Belgium.

2. The Abbey of Gethsemani is in Nelson County. The pioneers of whom Merton wrote settled in the part of Washington County that later became Marion County, Kentucky.

3. Today these are the Franciscan Sisters of Clinton, Iowa. When at Gethsemani, their novices went to Oldenburg, Indiana, for formation. When the sisters left Gethsemani, they went to Shelbyville, Kentucky, and later went west, to the Davenport, Iowa, diocese. For more information, see their website at www. clintonfranciscans.com/history.htm.

*Thomas Merton*

*Luke at her desk when she was superior general, photo from the mid-1960s*

Part II: Sr. Mary Luke Tobin on Merton

# Merton: Ten Years Later

## Editorial Note

This interview with Mary Luke Tobin was published in *Interchange,* the newsletter of the Loretto Community, on September 27, 1978. The introductory paragraph appeared at the beginning of the interview, which was conducted by Cecily Jones, SL, editor of the newsletter and Luke's long-time friend, housemate, and secretary.

## Text of the Interview

Later this fall, Sister Mary Luke Tobin will organize some discussion-evenings to begin the Thomas Merton Center for Creative Exchange in Denver. The opening of this Center will come near a time when, in many parts of this country and elsewhere, conferences and commemorations will mark the tenth anniversary of the death of Thomas Merton. He died in Bangkok, December 10, 1968. Sister Luke, who knew Merton well, will participate in several, giving talks or leading workshops: at Marquette University, Milwaukee, November 17; at Columbia University, New York City, November 27-December 8; at the University of Wisconsin, Madison, December 8-9. She has taught courses on Merton's thought at Iliff School of Theology in Denver and has been the consultant for Merton courses at Pendle Hill, Pennsylvania; she will give another course on Merton in the summer of 1979 at Iliff.

In this interview, Sister Luke answers questions about her acquaintance with Merton.

When did you first come to know Thomas Merton personally?

In 1960, when he came over to Loretto from Gethsemani to ask about the possibility of a teaching position on the Loretto Junior College faculty for his friend and former Columbia professor, Dan Walsh.[1] That began the years of Dr. Walsh's teaching philosophy to the novices, and it also led to a series of meetings and sharings with Thomas Merton.

He returned to Loretto, then, after that visit?

Yes, from time to time. He sometimes came to speak to the novices or to the retired sisters in the infirmary. On other occasions, he visited with a few members of the general council or just with one or two. Sometimes I visited Gethsemani and met with him to discuss current developments in religious life, prayer, the church, and so on.

What were some of the high points of the Loretto-Gethsemani connection?

You may remember that for our sesquicentennial in 1962 Thomas Merton wrote an essay on "Loretto and Gethsemani," which we used as the commemorative bulletin of our celebration at the motherhouse. He offered to do this for us. In the parallel stories of our two Kentucky centers—the Trappist monastery and our place at Loretto—he saw many aspects of similarity. Merton delighted in Loretto; he loved the old trees and hoped they would never have to come down. And he admired our buildings, especially the guest house as a striking example of simple architecture.

Apparently his interest in Loretto continued over the years?

That's right. His interest in our community and his willingness to share insights with us were a continuing source of inspiration and hope. Those who were in the novitiate then and who heard his talks will probably recall the good humor and sound common sense with which he developed themes of prayer and Christian commitment. He readily acceded to our requests for his expertise, either in answering questions or in meeting with small groups for discussion. ... [For example, at one of those meetings he said that he] greatly admired our guidelines in *I Am the Way*,[2] pointing out that he could add little to them and that he intended to talk with the other monks about them.

Some have spoken of the wide range of topics on which Merton wrote. Would you comment on this in the light of your acquaintance?

I found him a person of almost incredible intellectual interests. He had not only a very keen mind, but an enormous diversity of interests—ranging from the teachings of the Sufi masters to the writings of Marx, from the art of Zen to calligraphy to the Hasidic writers. Merton was an avid reader and would get excited about what he read; this prompted him to do his own probing. His journey to Asia (during which he died) was taken because he wanted to see where the search for the things of the spirit had led Eastern thinkers. He felt we could learn from them.

What were some of Merton's qualities for which you especially admired him?

I think Merton was very much a person for our time—a deeply committed Christian always searching in a profound way for answers to the perplexing problems of the day. Of course, I benefited by this probing into issues and by the exchanges we had.

Besides that, Thomas Merton was such a warm and simple human being—genuine, with nothing stuffy or artificial or arrogant about him.

I admired him, too, for his courage. He wrote open letters to the bishops about the nuclear threat, and often spoke out boldly about peace. Unafraid to call things by their right names, he saw into the fallacy of the arms race as the solution to world problems. In many ways, he was years ahead of his time.

Merton believed in each person's developing her/his goals with a maximum of freedom and a minimum of constraints, but always with the support of others standing by to be available when needed. A highlight of his teaching … was the importance of each one's freedom in the search for God and each one's faithfulness to the deepest insights of her/his pilgrimage. Merton himself accepted the framework of religious life, but held that this kind of freedom was essential to it. His words are on record to say that he himself never considered any different vocation.

What gave you the idea for starting the Thomas Merton Center for Creative Exchange?

I remember Merton's saying, during the last year of his life, "I'd like to see a center started where creative exchange could take place among contemplatives, activists, intellectuals, persons of various professions and disciplines, people whose ideas can help each other grow toward new insights. It could be located at Loretto, for example, and I'd be willing to help implement it." Of course, such a center was not begun at Loretto, and he did not live to facilitate it. I hope the Center, ten years later now, can help in some small way to develop this idea that Thomas Merton had.

Your exchanges with Merton would seem to put you in a unique role to begin such a center.

I do consider those years of sharing as priceless. During them, I received from Merton many mimeographed articles, which he autographed, a number of tapes, and so on. Because I've had this rich experience, I feel there are ways it could be shared.

Is there a new interest in Merton?

I think that an increasing number of people are interested in his thought and especially in his search. Many seem to be looking for a way in which their active responses to the critical issues of today can somehow be integrated with a life of faith.

What will happen at the Center?

In its very simple beginnings, we will hold "conversations" in living rooms. Since the Center takes its inspiration from Merton, each meeting will have as its theme a topic to which he devoted his thought. Many subjects he treated are especially relevant now. One example might be nuclear destruction ... or Faulkner's writings ... or Eastern religions. One person with special expertise will lead the discussion, opening it to the conversation of the wider group. Perhaps three evenings might be devoted to a single topic. I hope that in its quite modest way, the Center can provide opportunities for the kind of enriching exchange that Thomas Merton envisioned ten years ago.

## Editorial Afterword

Not long after its launching, the Thomas Merton Center for Creative Exchange expanded its offerings, moving from small discussion groups to an agenda of lectures, retreats, days of reflection, in which talks on Merton themes were often followed by discussions. To those looking for the Merton Center in a large building, Luke would smilingly explain that the Center was housed in her bedroom-office in her home, but that the Center's programs took place at several suitable facilities, such as Loretto Heights College, All Saints Church, St. Mary's Academy, Loretto Center, St. Thomas Seminary, all in the Denver area.

Dan Berrigan, SJ, gave the keynote talk at the formal opening of the Center (held at St. Mary's Academy, a Loretto-sponsored school). In the ensuing years, Luke engaged a litany of Merton scholars and spiritual leaders to conduct retreats and give presentations. A sampling of names includes William Shannon, Thomas Keating, OCSO, Jim Forest, Elena Malits, CSC, James Finley, Anthony Padovano, Bonnie Thurston, and James Conner, OCSO. Luke herself frequently led retreats and gave talks on Merton's thought and works.

In addition, Center offerings included the showing of films, including the one of Merton's final talk in Bangkok, the PBS documentary on Merton, and "Winter Rain," written by Anthony Padovano.

In October 1992, Luke transferred the leadership of the Merton Center to Rose Annette Liddell, SL. At that point in the Center's history, Luke wrote, "It has achieved much of its ongoing purpose: to forward the work of Thomas Merton, especially through retreats, exchanges, books, videos, and friendships." And that purpose continues to be fulfilled.

## Endnotes

1. Merton records this event in a journal entry on October 2, 1960. Victor D. Kramer, ed., *Turning Toward the World: The Journals of Thomas Merton* Volume

Four 1960-1963 (San Francisco: Harper San Francisco, 1997), 54-55.
    2. *I Am the Way* is the Constitutions of the Sisters of Loretto.

# Merton on Prayer: Start Where You Are[1]

## *By Mary Luke Tobin*

On a spring morning in 1963, the novices of the Sisters of Loretto in Kentucky were expecting an unusual visitor. The guest speaker for their class was to be their neighbor from Gethsemani, Thomas Merton, famous monk, poet, social critic, writer. Merton had graciously accepted the invitation to speak to the novices, which he agreed to do on more than one occasion, as a gesture of friendly sharing. His topic for the day was to be prayer.

The reflections which Merton presented to the Loretto novices are as fresh today as they were when he opened his discussion with them. It is worth noting that they are valid for laypersons as well as religious. One reads in these words practicality, understanding, and an invitation to the confidence which would lead the beginner forward with perseverance in the life of prayer. His advice was simple and useful:

> In prayer don't measure everything by your expectations when you're starting out.... You've got to be very realistic in the spiritual life—all through—but especially in prayer.
>
> Don't let your prayer be a fight against reality. And the first reality you've got is yourself, and that's where prayer begins. It begins with you and you don't have to go from you to God, because God is in you. All you've got to do is to stay where you are. You don't have to get out of this "base, earthly being" which you are and climb Jacob's ladder and get way up in the heavens where God is, because if you do that, you'll never pray. You couldn't pray.
>
> You have to start where you are and stay with it, because God is in you as you are, and doesn't expect you to be any other than you are, except that there is a change that God is going to make in your life. But you have to learn how to get together with God in your life so that this change can be made.
>
> There are two things you have to look out for, two extremes: on the one hand, an impractical idealism, and on the other hand, a sort of passive realism. The impractical idealism is the kind that says, "I've worked it out beforehand, and that's the way it's got to be." On the other hand, the wrong kind of realism says, "Well, this is the way it is, what can you do?" and just does nothing.
>
> Both these views are basically static, they never get anywhere. In between, there is the Christian view, which is: in the reality which I have and am now, there is a possibility for growth which God has

54

put there. There's a seed God has planted there and is going to make grow, and what I have to provide is the love and the assent that's going to permit it to grow.[2]

The novices heard these words of Thomas Merton with great interest, and took advantage of his encouragement to continue the session with questions his comments had provoked. Some of these, with his answers, follow:

What about distractions in prayer?

I used to try to pray by shutting out everything, and that was nice, but, of course, I was a novice. There used to be a man that lived down the back road, and I remember that the best part of my novitiate thanksgiving was this man going to work at the distillery. Every morning as he went down the back road, he whistled the same sort of tune, one of his own tunes, and you'd hear him coming. He always came at the same time, and for some reason or another, that was a wonderful thing in that thanksgiving. Here was the world. Here was this lonely man on the back road, and it meant a great deal.

Merton drew another example from nature:

Our place at Gethsemani is full of birds. You simply listen to every one of the birds individually, which is heresy according to the spiritual books, for it's a deliberate distraction. Actually, it's a wonderful thanksgiving, because who made those birds, and who put them there, and who is making them sing, and who is the source of their life? It is the one who is in my heart and is the source of my life, and I'm one with all those things.

Where do the world's happenings fit into prayer?

You know, if we can get out of ourselves and think of the things that are going on in the world, the issues that are so important in the world, we're really not distracted. The trouble is that some people are taught to regard those things as distractions. They are not. We should have compunction today for collective crime, because there's where compunction is called for.

Merton consistently taught that compunction (the prick of conscience) is profoundly connected with our complicity with social sin:

We're called upon to have compunction because of the nuclear bombs, etc. For this we should have deep compunction; also for racism, and for the whole war-peace issue. I really think that in our life of prayer, as far as I'm concerned, this question of distraction is gone when you get down to these big issues. You haven't got time to be distracted, because you realize that we're living in the age of the concentration camp and the threat of nuclear war, etc.

Sometimes prayer is difficult. Sometimes you can't pray.

Well, prayer is work, but it's a very special kind of delicate work in which we have to let God work; the dead spots in prayer are very important. The fact that you may not be able to pray for days on end doesn't matter; it may be worthwhile. It's just like the winter in the life of a plant. The plants aren't wasting time in the winter; they're not losing anything. Winter is very important for the plants, and these periods of stillness and incapacity may be, actually, the best things in your life of prayer.

These thoughts of Merton, shared with the novices, laid a sort of foundation for prayer. Prayer should begin with reality, with one's identity, avoiding idealism and passivity, and should be open to nature and to the world of struggle and social sin. The dead spots in prayer are important.

The Loretto novices were fortunate to have occasional instructions from their famous visitor. Other students also gathered notes from Thomas Merton's lectures, notably the novices at Gethsemani, where he was their director. These particular notes emphasize relationships with the neighbor within the total reality:

If we are attentive to what is, we are attentive to God and God is touching us in what is (reality). If you are with God, you see God in everything and everyone…. All creatures are the place where God's love is manifested…. Prayer is a social art.

We get into direct contact with God by our relationship with people. It is in the concrete situations in life that the will of God is expressed.

Later on, in the mid-1960s, there were other occasions to speak with Merton on the topic of prayer. On a fine July day, two or three of us went to meet him at the lake at Gethsemani.[3] I recall the scene: the warm Kentucky sun was reflected in the sparkling water. Merton was seated on the concrete wall of the dam. We were asking him questions about prayer.

"Well, you see, prayer is basically response," he said. "In prayer we are continually responding to the questions of who we are and who God is. We're working with reality here—the reality of our own identity and freedom and its relationship to God."

As his words indicate, prayer for Merton is a way of finding one's true identity, one's true self. In conferences at Gethsemani, he spoke about it this way:

> Prayer has but one function: to bring us to a personal awareness of
> our oneness with God in Christ…. We will achieve awareness only
> if we discover our true self, ground of our being…. Seeking God
> with our whole heart is finding God within us; and where we are
> there God is.

Prayer helps you find your identity, your true self united with God. In
this identity, you find your freedom; and in this freedom, you are able
to respond to reality. For me, one of Merton's clearest descriptions of
this relationship between identity, freedom, and reality is expressed in a
lecture to the Gethsemani community:

> One of the purposes of the ascetical life is freedom. Freedom to do
> what you really want. And what do you really want? To be able to
> love without impediment! To be free to do what in the depths of your
> heart you really want to do. To be free to love what is important, what
> is worthy of our freedom as sons [and daughters] of God.
>
> The real question is not "Am I happy?" but "Am I free?" Am I
> developing the freedom God has given me, the freedom to respond
> with my whole self to reality, to what is. Asceticism frees us from
> depending on external conditions or on others in responding to reality
> and happiness. All that stuff which comprises our "false self," what
> I like or dislike, my attitudes, etc., is not important. What is true and
> lasting is deeper than this false self; asceticism helps us to live on
> that deep level of the true self.
>
> God is identified with our inner self which remains even if every-
> thing is taken away. Everything can be gone, but God is in our center
> and that center is all that is left when we die. Real freedom is to be
> able to come and go to that center. When we die, everything (false
> self) is destroyed except that which is important, the true, inner self,
> the center. The only thing that is important is this inner reality, for
> God preserves and is identified with it. Nobody can touch or hurt this
> center. We must be free to be in contact with this center.

So important is this rootedness in reality that Merton believes there is no
prayer and no interior life without it. "The interior life is what happens
to you when you come alive in contact with reality," he says. "You do
not come in contact with God except through reality. The interior life is
the capacity to respond. Prayer is not praying five or six times a day. It
is an expression of who we are."

Merton believes that prayer, meditation, and contemplation should not be placed in distinctly separate compartments. In his discussion of prayer, he often interchanges these terms to emphasize such a conviction.

The purpose of meditation, Merton says, is establishing contact with God in a union which is a font of life, truth, and reality:

> Meditation gets us rooted in reality. At the end of a meditation we should have *more* being, be more real, than when we started. This is not a matter of feeling, but of faith.

He adds:

> We should be open to God in meditation. When your heart is in a simple, quiet awareness, then that is meditation. An awareness is realizing that God has loved us in a special way. Once you have tasted this awareness, everything else is trivial and your life gets a new orientation. Your heart is awake; it is loving.
>
> Prayer is not reasoning, it is intuitive, relaxed, letting go, collapsing into God.

In writing specifically about contemplation, Merton insists on the importance of being awake to reality. He taught that contemplation is integrated with all of life, and spoke of the "now" as the real moment of prayer. Here, in particular, I believe, his reflections reveal Zen influence.

William Shannon in his book *Thomas Merton's Dark Path* comments that "Merton suggests a type of prayer that has some kinship with authentic Zen meditation in that it seeks an intuition of being beyond the dualities of life. Like Zen, it is an integrating prayer in which one finds the center of one's life, one's 'original self' (as Zen practitioners would put it). It differs, however, from Zen in that Merton would see that center as rooted in God."[4]

Merton describes Christian mysticism: "Contemplation is the awareness and realization, even in some sense experience, of what each Christian obscurely believes: 'It is now no longer I that live, but Christ lives in me.'" Merton suggests Zen influence as he explains, "Meditation has no point and no reality unless it is firmly rooted in life."[5]

In searching for an explanation of this kind of integrating prayer, Merton uses many images and symbols rather than one specific definition. In *New Seeds of Contemplation*, his descriptions are truly poetic:

> Contemplation is nothing less than life itself fully awake, fully alive, fully aware that it is alive.[6]

We can see that Merton does not intend these statements as definitions. He is trying to explain what in reality is indefinable.

In *New Seeds*, Merton describes contemplation as a state of "heightened consciousness, the highest expression of the intellectual and spiritual life, spontaneous awe of the sacredness of life, of being; gratitude for life, for awareness, and for being; a breakthrough to a new level of reality: vivid awareness of the reality of the sources of life and being; an awakening to the Real within all that is real."[7]

Does Merton give any practical suggestions for the one who wishes to respond? Merton was indeed a practical man, and never left the student of prayer without some helps or hints about the path ahead. For example, Merton invites learners to find their own method of praying with "an awakened heart" and to stay with it.

The great study of the one who wishes to pray is to have an "awakened heart" to cultivate an awareness of the love of God, a continuous, quiet, humble desire for God; not a concept of God which involves strain or an idea of God, rather a general openness, awareness of God. This keeps your heart awake. Find something that suits you, find your own formula and do it spontaneously, working, walking, etc. You don't have to be telling yourself, "I am praying," or even know it. Don't reflect on yourself or be too conscious of it. Just do it. And if it works for you, spend the rest of your life doing it.

He speaks of a "kind of doing nothing which is extremely fruitful, as long as you are there. You have to be present, not daydreaming. All these things you have to learn by trial and error."

An ever greater simplicity appears in Merton's later observations on prayer. One notices his direct, to-the-point comments, without wordiness, long explanations, formality. His instructions dealt with a profound subject, but in a very simple manner.

In the final years of Merton's life, he gathered together at Gethsemani a group of prioresses of contemplative orders.[8] He felt he needed to help these women create a freer and more human climate for the life of prayer in their communities. He could see that they were impeded by some of the restrictive rules and requirements put on them by the male superiors of their orders. Merton invited me to participate in those meetings.

I was happy to share in the warmth, freedom, and spontaneity which he generated among these sisters. He took for granted that they affirmed the life of contemplation, and assumed that they saw it as he did. Always he was conscious of the need to help not only these women but all students of prayer to arrive at an experience where the duality between God and ourselves disappears.

Merton emphasized in his teachings that where contemplation becomes what it is really meant to be "it is no longer something infused by God into a created subject so much as it is God living in God and identifying a created life with his own life so that there is nothing left of any significance but of God living in God."

The whole essence of contemplative prayer, he said, is that the division between subject and object disappears. "You do not look at God as an object nor at yourself as an object. You don't stand back and look at yourself. You are just not interested in yourself."

In his comments to the contemplative nuns, Merton urges them to realize that God's concern is not the false self, not one's faults. Indeed, God takes care of that, Merton insists:

> Don't worry about that false self. God is carrying these faults with you and for you. They're not important to God. In our struggle with ourselves we have a choice—hope or despair. And, of course, the despairing choice is: "God could not possibly live in someone like me." The other choice is to turn back to God again as to the ground of our being, the root of our life, the source from which our life comes. And that is our prayer. This is a pattern of prayer; it is not something we do. It's something we are. The struggle itself is our existence.
>
> If someone comes to me and says, "How do I pray?" I can give some suggestions about recollection, acts of faith, breathing, etc. Basically, that's not really telling them anything. What I have to say is that actually your prayer is getting to realize that the very struggle which is the basis of your existence is prayer. And that you are praying as long as you exist and don't run away from the center of your being.
>
> This business of constantly struggling to return to the center is your prayer. True contemplatives are those who live with this constant orientation, ultimately realizing that they have to be always returning to the one source of their being, which is Christ, who is identified with them, and is their being. You cannot be without your source; it's there. Even if you are divided off from Christ, you can nevertheless return to him because he's there.

This simplicity continued in Merton's later words. He spent less and less time teaching about prayer and gave more and more encouragement to his listeners to "simply pray." In one of his last talks to the Gethsemani community he said:

> One of the reasons I don't like to talk about prayer much is that it is not good to make a great issue out of prayer. It should be as simple as breathing and living. As soon as you make an issue out of it, it tends to get confused and distorted. Prayer should be neither sacred

nor secular. I don't regard prayer as a specifically sacred activity. It is life. It is our life and comes from the ground of our life. We should not divide prayer against the rest of our lives. Prayer should be the activity in which we are most ourselves because we are aware of our identity as children of God and we live in this relationship to God.

The same insistence on simplicity appears in Merton's talks about prayer to a gathering in Redwoods, Calif.[9] A friend of mine present at the conference quotes from Merton's reflections there:

> The only valid life of prayer is where Christ is praying. His prayer in you is the quickest way to forget you are praying. Yet you still have to *want* to pray. You have to start with your illusory self. But prayer is not just a human action; it is a response to the Spirit. Our whole life then becomes praise…. Not that I thank him, but *I am thanks, praise*. Christ is. There's no need to knock to get in. You are in.
>
> Prayer is praying? No. Prayer is turning to God within you? Yes.

Both at Redwoods and in Asia, Merton insisted that we really have all we need for a life of prayer. One could say such a conviction is the very essence of simplicity:

> In prayer, we discover what we already have. You start where you are and you deepen what you already have. And you realize you are already there. We now have everything, but we don't know it, and we don't experience it. Everything has been given to us in Christ. All we need is to experience what we really possess. If we truly want prayer, we'll have to give it time. We must slow down to a human tempo and we'll begin to have time to listen.[10]

In this statement, Merton cuts through to the heart of the matter, awareness of God's presence at the center of each person. This understanding is never more evident than in Merton's final expressions on prayer.

His last talk was given in Bangkok. Here, after he had spoken to Asian monks and nuns, he was reproved by a listener who wondered why he hadn't talked more about converting people to Christianity. He replied that in the life of prayer, as in the Christ life, "being" is more important than "saying." He spoke these words: "What we are asked to do at present is not so much to speak of Christ as to let him live in us so that people may find him by feeling how he lives in us."

In this remark, Merton sums up for us his teaching on prayer. He has shown how prayer must deal with reality; that one's life struggle itself is prayer; that prayer lives and grows at the Center where the true self recognizes its identity in God; that gradually one learns to pray "without dualism"; and that finally all one's life is expressed by the sentence, "I live now, not I, but Christ lives in me."[11]

## Endnotes

1. *Praying*, No. 1, *National Catholic Reporter*, 1984. Where possible, the editors have cited Sr. Luke's sources.

2. From Merton's talk of May 15, 1963, reproduced in Part I of this book. Many quotations in this essay are from that talk.

3. Merton records a July 23, 1968, meeting with "Sister Luke and four others from Loretto" for Mass and conversation by the lake. Patrick Hart, OCSO, ed., *The Other Side of the Mountain: The Journals of Thomas Merton* Volume Seven1967-1968 (San Francisco: Harper San Francisco 1998), 145.

4. William H. Shannon, *Thomas Merton's Dark Path* (Revised ed.)(New York: Farrar, Straus, Giroux, 1981/87), 125-126.

5. It is unclear whether Luke continues to quote *Dark Path*.

6. Sr. Luke here paraphrases the opening of *New Seeds of Contemplation* (New York: New Directions, 1961), 1.

7. *New Seeds*, 3.

8. An account of these meetings appears in Jane Marie Richardson, ed., *The Springs of Contemplation* (New York: Farrar, Straus, Giroux, 1992).

9. We do not know Sr. Luke's "source," but one account of this event was written by Br. David Steindl-Rast, OSB, "Recollections of Thomas Merton's Last Days in the West," *Monastic Studies* 7 (1969): 1-10. Br. David also contributed a chapter to Br. Patrick Hart's *Thomas Merton, Monk* (New York: Sheed and Ward, 1994), "Man of Prayer," which records Merton's teaching in California.

10. Almost this exact quotation occurs in Br. David Steindl-Rast's chapter, "Man of Prayer," 80.

11. Galatians 2:20.

# Prayer and Commitment in Thomas Merton[1]

*The following is the transcript of a talk given
by Mary Luke Tobin.*

We may think that this is a man who died in 1968 and here we are more than 20 years away from that.… I would say that Merton is better known today and more widely respected today than ever before. One little testimony of that: where I live in Denver there is a very excellent book store, and it is a beautiful and extensive book store and has many new books coming up all the time. I remember when I first started to set up a center in Denver about 12 years ago I went over there to get some Merton books. It was not particularly a religious bookstore, more a universal bookstore.… They had about four or five—maybe half a shelf—of Merton's books there, and I could select some that I couldn't get anywhere else there. Today if you go you'll find four shelves of Merton's books. That illustrates something. In the past ten years the growth that has happened. Why do people seek out Merton? He had a message that all of us want to hear. We want to expand not only our knowledge of Merton, but expand his own growth and development as we begin to understand and to know more about him. He is one who said of himself, "Don't read my books from five or six years ago. They are already outdated."

Well, actually they aren't outdated. But one nevertheless sees a difference in Merton's thought as he himself grew older, and I think it is well to understand that, when you are reading Merton,… it is always a good idea to realize: here is a man growing, but growing from a tradition, growing from a deep insight which was his from the very beginning of his beginning to write in a certain light. And so for that reason I think we have to balance both of those. Either something he is saying is from the depths of the tradition, never grows old, or something he is saying from that depth again but aspects of it fit a more current theme. Again and again he has indicated both of those things. He wants to reach the audience of today, but he wants to reach them with the richest things in the tradition. So you will find that going on with him. He doesn't abandon the tradition at all. No way does he abandon it. But he also sorts it out. The tradition itself is the everlasting. The changing times do reflect in different ways on that tradition and peel away from it those things that are quite prime conditions. Merton is doing that, I think, in most of his writings.

I want to start today's reflections on Merton and prayer and commitment with a little quote from the new autobiography of the Dalai Lama. The Dalai Lama, as you know, the great Tibetan leader, driven out of his country with many of his monks, thousands of them really, and living in exile today in India, widely traveled, has just come out with his autobiography.[2] He says a couple of things about Thomas Merton in that autobiography that I want to begin with. Merton met with the Dalai Lama in 1968, a short time before his death, and was deeply impressed by the man.[3] The impressions were mutual, and this is what the Dalai Lama has to say about those meetings. He says, "One of my happiest memories of this time is the occasion when I was fortunate enough to receive a visit from Father Thomas Merton, the American Benedictine monk [we would specify Trappist today although certainly Benedictine]. He came to Dharamsala in November 1968, just a few weeks before his tragic death in Thailand. We met on three consecutive days, for two hours at a time. Merton was a well-built man of medium height, with even less hair than me, [so he might be even a little easier to caricature, maybe] though that was not because his head was shaved as mine is. He had big boots and wore a thick leather belt around the middle of his heavy, white cassock. But more striking than his outward appearance, which was memorable in itself, was the inner life that he manifested. I could see he was a truly humble and deeply spiritual man. This was the first time that I had been struck by such a feeling of spirituality in anyone who professed Christianity. Since then, I have come across others with similar qualities, but it was Merton who introduced me to the real meaning of the word 'Christian.'"[4]

All those take note who think that Merton moved away from Christianity into Buddhism or something like that. It was Merton who introduced the great Buddhist, the Dalai Lama, to Christianity, and I think it is a wonderful witness that this is said here. "Our meetings were conducted in a very pleasant atmosphere. Merton was both humorous and well informed. I called him a Catholic *geshe* [expert wisdom teacher]. We talked about intellectual and spiritual matters that were of mutual interest and exchanged information about monasticism. [The Dalai Lama is a monk, a Buddhist monk.] I was keen to learn all that I could about the monastic tradition in the West. He told me a number of things that surprised me, notably that Christian practitioners of meditation do not adopt any particular physical position when they meditate."[5] Now the Dalai Lama was surprised at this because it is part of the description of meditation in most of the Eastern religions, certainly Buddhism, to have a particular posture. That surprised him. But it doesn't surprise *us* who know that meditation, prayer, contemplation, spirituality, is wider in its concept, includes all day every day. And he says, "According to my understanding, position and even breathing are vital components to its practice."[6] Merton would affirm that, of course, and say that breathing practices were part of his own meditation…. The last thing I wanted to read about him [the Dalai

Lama] is this: "All together it was a useful exchange—not least because I discovered from it that there are many similarities between Buddhism and Catholicism. So I was extremely sad to hear of his sudden death. Merton acted as a strong bridge between our two very different religious traditions. [I'd like to underline that.] Above all, he helped me to realise that every major religion, with its teaching of love and compassion, can produce good human beings."[7]

I really wanted to read it because I think Merton shows in this quote how his own search for how religion and prayer and spirituality experienced in different traditions of the whole world make it possible for us to stand and enrich our own understanding in our own faith tradition of the life of contemplation, meditation, prayer—all three of which Merton interchanged continually.

So I would like to talk today about some of Merton's teachings on prayer. I am going to do this chronologically because it struck me…that, if you look at Merton in different periods of his life, you will see some differences, and you will see some constants, some variables and some constants. And I'd like to start out with one of the constants. It seems to me that what Merton insisted upon in any teaching of spirituality, of prayer, was a profound fact about identity. Merton wanted the one who was going to pray to know who he or she is, to search for those deep wellsprings within one that enable one to come more to an understanding of who one is. That is what Merton was after. That is the constant that goes through all of his writings, all of his thought. Who are we really? Merton thought, as I like to express in the words of Karl Rahner, another great theologian of our times, "every human being is an event of the absolute, radical, free self-communication of God." So insofar as Merton saw that every human person, every human person—not just Catholics, Christians, Jews, Buddhists, Hindus, agnostics, atheists—every human person is "an event of the absolute, free, radical self-communication of God." That's the basic concept. That is what Merton, in everything he writes, is either explaining and expressing or taking for granted that one knows. His teaching on prayer and spirituality flows from that deep underlying rock bed, granite solidity of the marvelous experience of all of us. Whether we don't realize, don't know—that we are events of God's self-communication, God communicates God's self to us. We have no idea of our stature. We have no idea of our greatness. One of the French philosophers made the statement: All love is luck. The more you think about it, the truer it seems.

All love is luck. And the luck that we have as human beings is that God communicates God's self to us every time at all times. It's that greatness that we lose sight of when we fasten onto our individual faults or our imperfections, or whatever we may fasten onto that threatens us, rather than who we really are and that that greatness will be with us always. Merton expressed that very beautifully in one of his early writings when he said God identifies God's self with us.[8] And when we die, the only thing that will be left is the self-identification of ourselves with God. Now that's not pantheistic. We don't read "I am God." That is not at all what Merton is saying. Merton is saying that God communicates God's self to us, and that's what is left when we die, not something else left over, but that one thing. Everything else is taken away, says Merton, but that profound sense, that profound reality rather, of God's identification with us. God sees fit to so identify God's self with us.

I was very lucky during the sixties, all during the sixties, to have contact with Thomas Merton because he lived just twelve miles away, and so on many occasions he came over to our place, or I went over to his place, to talk about something that was of mutual interest, to talk about the things of the time, to talk about the Church and its evolution, to talk about many things that I was involved in with the questions of religious congregations, and that he was involved in not only in that way but in his worldwide outlook. So it was a very rich time for me, and I cannot tell you how happy I am to share any of those experiences that came to me through Merton.

I was thinking the other day—people bring around relics to places and I thought, "What relic now.... I knew Thomas Merton and had talked with him like that, so what would I bring, something I could pass around?" Then I thought, "There are autographed books, he autographed a lot of books for me. No, I don't think that would be the thing. Bob Daggy has thousands of them down there at the center."[9] And then I thought, "I know what I could pass around," and you'd be very surprised. I didn't actually bring this, but I could well do it if I were into that kind of thing.

When I was in South America one time because we had missions there, I said to Merton before I left, "What would you like to have brought back to you from South America?" "Oh," he says, "you can bring me a reed flute." And I thought, that shouldn't be too hard to get and so, although I got a reed flute, he had other reed flutes, but while I was in South America somebody gave me something that I brought back to Thomas Merton. It was a little bottle, a liqueur bottle, and the particular liqueur that was in the bottle was named *Juan de la Cruz*. John of the Cross liqueur! I'll bring him this little bottle of *Juan de la Cruz* liqueur. And believe me, he was delighted. He made the most of it and loved it. In fact, he hung it up in his hermitage in the lattice wall between the kitchen and the living room of his hermitage. There I saw it a couple of times, hanging on a little string, this little bottle of *Juan de la Cruz* liqueur. And so when the hermitage was dismantled, and Brother Patrick Hart asked me what I wanted out of the hermitage, I said, "One thing. That little bottle that is hanging on the lattice work between the two…." He gave it to me. I should have brought it and passed it around to you. Next time I'll do that. But it gives you something of the fanciful which was always deeply appreciated and the wholeness of Merton who would certainly have appreciated *Juan de la Cruz* himself and in this case *Juan de la Cruz* liqueur. And there's where he kept it until his death.

I mention that simply because I know that relics are sometimes thought of as belonging to an older age of the church. We don't talk much about relics today. And when I was in Rome at the Vatican Council, one of the persons canonized at that time was a monk named Charbel.[10] Charbel was Lebanese, and he was a hermit. When I heard he was going to be canonized while we were there at Vatican II, I wrote to Merton and said, "Do you want a relic of Charbel, because there is a nun here from Lebanon who can get us one?" And he wrote back immediately, "Of course, I would love one! I am a great relic man myself!"[11] And so before we erase those things as totally from the past, let's make in a sense a kind of reverence of those persons who seemed to have touched somewhere that we are aspiring to. It's a lovely thing to have some memory of them. I didn't really plan to tell you this, but there it was; it sprang up in my mind.

What Merton says in one of his talks or in the little notebook that he prepared for his novices at the very beginning, I think it's expressive of what I just said about identity being the heart of Merton's message on prayer or on anything else. In the little preface to a book on prayer that he did for the novices, he put it this way: "Prayer is not only the lifting up of the mind and heart to God, but it is also the response to God within us, the discovery of God within us. It leads ultimately to the discovery and fulfillment of our own created being in God."[12] And so Merton there expresses this identity and tells us that not only is prayer lifting up to God, but looking within, finding God within us, and responding. So prayer in one way is responding. I think he puts that then in very clear language in this particular little piece.

I wanted to talk about the times that I was with Merton or knew him and when he talked about prayer in particular, and I'd like to do it chrono-logically and to start out with what things Merton was saying in the first years that I knew. I met him in 1960 and then all during the sixties I knew him. One day he came over to our house, and I asked him if he would talk to the novices, the young women preparing to become sisters. They were there, and he did a fine presentation, of course, as he would, lively, full of interest to them and full of events of the times which he always wove in when he talked about prayer or anything else.

On this particular day he was talking to the novices about prayer and something about how to prepare yourself for it. After he got home and began to think about it, which happened several times, he would say to himself (and we've all had this experience, I am sure—I know what I should have said), he would go back, and he would either write you a letter or he would say something about it in which you could see that he was himself trying to pick up on that insight that he had from the day before. That happened in this early period of 1961[13] and he goes through a little experience of that, and I'd like to share a little bit of that because if we are talking about prayer I think we have something very particular here.

I was with the novices and Sister Helen Jean was with the novices when he was talking with them, and he addresses the letter to her and he said, "I didn't say all I would like to have said about prayer. I think prayer supposes some kind of training, some kind of training that would not be just theologically in a vacuum. There must be some kind of basic training such as this way." He says, "In training for mental prayer, the real training, the … discipline, and learning is how to exercise oneself in different ways."[14] Now Merton in his talks to his own novices always said, "The purpose of the ascetical life, the disciplined life, is freedom. Because as we begin to move through an ascetical life, it's so we can say 'yes' and 'no' when we want to." Marvelous introduction. The purpose of the ascetical life is freedom so that when we choose to say "no," we can say "no"; when we choose to say "yes," we can say "yes." The addictive society in which we live today could learn a lot from that. The ability to choose, the chance to choose and to say "yes" or "no" to opportunities offered--it takes some kind of training and discipline to be able to do that. That's what he is talking about. He sort of laid it down as a first principle here. So he wants them to have this ability.

Merton was very good at saying "on the one hand—on the other"—a man of great balance, not in the sense that neither one is right or wrong but in a sense of paradox. It seems to me that when we hold two contradictory intentions long enough we find out that maybe they are not contradictory, maybe we have simply expanded our own circumference wide enough to allow both of them to exist. And Merton could do that. He could see the good in both sides of many arguments, and therefore he wants them [the novices] in preparation for prayer to be able to do this. So not that they will know how to meditate if they practice it differently, but so that they don't get the idea that they know how to meditate. That was the other side of it for him. That's the second thing he wrote to Helen Jean, so that they don't claim a thing so tightly that they never know when to let go. So Merton's prayer was always a kind of balance between some profound truth, some profound insight, and the ability to let go, following the pattern, reading the scriptures. And in the letter to Sister Helen Jean he emphasizes reading the scriptures is an important part because the scriptures are so broad, and they contain so much human truth that we never tire, and should never tire of exploring them. "The pleasant fields of the scriptures" as Therese of Lisieux used to say. "When I get my head bogged down and my head busy filled with so many intellectual ideas, I turn to the pleasant fields of the scriptures." Merton suggested the scriptures give the kind of perspective that is needed.

Merton did not have a method of prayer. Sometimes you hear "Oh, yes, this method—that's Merton's method." Merton didn't have a method. He was too open for that, and he felt also that every person had his or her own way of approaching prayer, and it was according to one's personality. Dom John Chapman of England made the statement: "Don't pray as you can't, pray as you can." It was a good human rule, and Merton would have affirmed that solidly, that one prays as one can, according to one's own characteristics. Therefore, he said, "They have to learn when to let go and when not to." [15] A balance, and there are no prayer rules for this, said Merton. It has to be according to the individual, and I think that's why he didn't set up "the Thomas Merton method of prayer." Thank God he didn't! He left it wide open to us in all the ways we can explore the wonderful things he said about prayer without being pinned down to one particular type of prayer called "Thomas Merton type of prayer." He would have laughed at that and said that is too narrow and doesn't belong to the way God leads us all in prayer.

And then the curse of meditation…is watching ourselves. How am I doing? I did better today. Watching oneself meditate. Just become aware of the fact that there are many things one can do in meditation without doing any one of them very much. It's good to know how much one can fall back on in a crisis. But go along without relying on methods—these are Merton's words to Helen Jean—but on God, God's self, provided one's faith is enough to permit this. So there has to be some maturity before one can get to that. He wanted more time with the novices, and he said they taught him more than he taught them. That's a typical Merton thing.

So the first thing I would suggest is that you can find a copy of what I just said in the new book, *The School of Charity,* to find that little passage on Merton's instruction to the novices. Merton instructed his own novices continually because they needed the same thing he was always able to give them. That was the first thing. Later on in 1963 I had a chance to invite Merton to talk to the novices again.[16] "Start where you are," says Merton. "Be realistic." He presented the novices with two ideas, and he said there are two sides of the dilemma that we can go to one or to the other and miss out on something. This is the way he describes them. He says: Don't let your prayer be a flight from reality. The first reality you've got is yourself and that is where prayer begins.... You don't have to go from you to God. God is already with you. You don't have to go up some Jacob's ladder to God. God's there at all times.

It reminds us of Merton's definition of contemplation in *New Seeds*.[18] Contemplation is an awareness, an awakening to the Real within all that is real. A beautiful way to put the relationship of God to the whole world. Actually, Merton talks about two things here in his descriptions. The first thing is flight from reality, flight from yourself. If you don't learn to know who you are, you have to stay where you are; you've got it all right there. All luck is love. All love is luck. It's all right there. You've got it. We don't have to get out of it and climb Jacob's ladder and get way up to the heavens where God is. Because if you do, you'll never pray. You couldn't pray. Start where you are and stay with it, because God is in you where you are and doesn't expect you to be any other than you are, except for the change that God is going to bring about in you.

I think what Merton was saying in 1963 is this change that God is bringing about is continual in all of us. You have to learn how to get together with God in your life so that the change can be made. And he said these are the two things to look out for. First, an *impractical idealism* and second, a *passive realism*. Now you can get that from his illustration. He says the impractical idealism is the kind that says "I worked it all out before and that's the way it's got to be." Impractical idealism. The wrong kind of realism says, "Well, this is the way it is. What can you do?" And does nothing. Most of these views, Merton says, ... never get anywhere. In between is the Christian view which is: in the reality which I have and which I am now, there is a possibility for growth which God has put there. There is a seed God has planted there and is going to make grow, and what I have to provide is the love and the assent that is going to permit it to grow. And so Merton tells these young novices, these young women, that are in Kentucky in 1963, two things to watch out for: steer clear of both that idealism and realism and stay in the middle with what you have which is already yours, and be trusting yourself about what God is going to bring about.

He tells us again that, when they asked him a question about distractions, he said there really are no distractions, if you want to look at this from God's view. There is much need for compunction, the spirit of great regret, even mourning. He is not talking about personal guilt when he is talking about that, and I think that is a wise thing. Not personal guilt that things are as they are, but in a way, that things are this bad, and Merton didn't want that excluded from one's prayer life. Merton wanted us to consider that and realize the little we can do about it, nevertheless. We are living, as Merton says, in the age of concentration camps, the threat of nuclear war, and today the list goes on to say the threat of war caused by our own greed. Merton would have been in to every one of these ways of looking at it. He would look at the world in every one of these ways and tell us that we *have* to think about it.[17]

All right, I'd like to think, too, that Merton saw prayer as not specifically sacred. It comes from the ground of our life. We should not divide our prayer, says Merton, from the rest of our lives. It is too integral, the activity in which we are most ourselves, he goes on to say. And so actually that is what he was saying in 1963 and again, not too different, the same profound principles we hold today.

Let's move on a little bit age-wise and move into Merton in 1965 and 1966. In those years—they were the years when he had achieved what he had been longing for so long, life in the hermitage, life alone. He was able to write again in so many ways in those years, profoundly influenced by his new insight as he began to look East and incorporate into much of his life what he had learned from Asian monasticism or from the writings of the great Asians. So the things he is writing for his own novices are many of the things that are said. He was influenced not only by Buddhists, that was a special concentration, as you know, of his last years…but also by other eastern religions. He was very impressed by that mystic tradition in Islam which is the tradition of the Sufis.

The Sufi tradition, rich as it was, had much to speak to Merton. Some of his best comments on the tapes are things that he was learning from the Sufis as well as from the Buddhists. And from the Sufis he had a great love for what they had to say about prayer of the heart.[19] And while encouraging us to use the Christian prayer of the heart, he wanted to extend and deepen and enrich our sense of prayer by incorporating and learning about some of those things from the East. He certainly saw the Jesus prayer, *Jesus, Son of the living God, have mercy on me, a sinner*, as an enormously important Christian prayer, and he encouraged people to use it over and over again. He was devoted to the Rosary. He always had a Rosary in his possession and used it. I was talking to some people the other day and they said "but the Rosary is so Catholic" whereas today we are learning about scripture. I said, "Wait! Wait! 90% of the Rosary is scripture!" Besides scripture, it's what you pray for. Other than that, it is all scripture. Well, it doesn't hurt to treat scripture as the Rosary does. Merton was devoted to that. It is a constant prayer.

But when he got to the Sufis, he learned something that could be incorporated into our whole sense of prayer. The Sufis talk about the prayer of the heart, and many of Merton's talks on the Sufi tradition in the early part of 1968 and the end of 1967 had to do with what he was learning from the Sufis.[20] Sufism looks at a human person as a heart and a spirit and as a secret. The secret is the deepest part. The secret of the human being is God's secret. Therefore, it is in God. My secret is God's innermost knowledge of me which God alone possesses. God's secret knowledge of God's self in me, of myself in God, which is a beautiful concept. The heart is the faculty by which a human person knows God and therefore Sufism develops the heart.

Merton says (this is very biblical) the spirit is almost the same as the biblical "word," spirit…the breath of life, the Sufi expression—the breath of life, the spirit. So one knows God with one's heart, but loves God with one's life. It is your living self that is an act of constant love to God, and this inmost secret of a person is that by which he or she contemplates God, which is the secret of a person in God's concept. This is a very, very deep concept of man, says Merton, and some day I hope to go further with it. And then he says, the Sufis have a beautiful development of what the secret really is. It is the word "yes." And the act of "yes." It is a secret affirmation which God places in my heart, a "yes" to God. That's God's secret. God knows my name even when I'm not saying it. My destiny in life, final inspiration, is to uncover this "yes" so that my life is totally and completely an assent to God. When you see the contemplative life in that sense, you can see how it works together with a life of action or whatever else. It is while constantly saying "yes" that the contemplative life is an inner "yes" itself. So when Merton is extolling the monastic life in its setting, by which he learned to say "yes," he is saying a complete "yes" to God, is known by God, is the secret, the complete "yes" to God.

Merton says that God gives us the potential for saying this yes—we're not only conscious of saying it. Merton speaks of a holy spot that resides in you, which again is an analogy, a symbol, which you may fan into a consuming flame which will burn away the dross, the unworthiness, and sin. That spot of holiness is the "yes" which, according to the Sufis, you cannot ever extinguish. And Merton quickly says, "This is also the Christian view." This is the most profound meaning of our personalities which is that we say "yes" to God, and the spot is always there. All we need to do is turn toward it and let it become a flame. This is the way we are made, and our lives should be built on this conception of the human person which we do not find in ordinary psychology. There are almost infinite potentialities in this concept, and what we have to learn is that we are learning about prayer to learn to develop them.

If someone is living in an unconditional YES to God's love, he or she is fully living what they come to understand religion to be for. Nothing else really matters, once that is taken care of. Everybody can do this—not just monks, nuns, people in religious life. It is simply a Christian way of life. For us, everything else should be stripped away so we're actually more constantly and more continually in this spirit. I think as Merton grew into 1967 and 1968, he became intrigued with various ideas, and then he developed them. He learned them from the different religions of the world, and he also learned them from many of the great thinkers of the world.

One of the ideas that we find expressed in Merton's last years, 1967 and 1968, is this idea of alienation.[21] It has certainly implications here, how one becomes separated from one's true self and how one becomes, for instance, a slave to somebody else or something else, and therefore one is not able to make one's own decisions. That is what alienation is about. It splits the self into two parts: that which somebody else tells you to do, somebody else's idea, somebody else's way of acting, and you adopt it as if it were yours. You become influenced.

Now I don't have to tell you much about the influence of our culture in that regard, especially consumerism. We are totally influenced, or at least greatly influenced, by the culture around us that persuades us what we will buy and how much we will have. So consumerism is a great enemy of the true self, the self that is united, so that it can really choose. To be able really to choose, you need not only the discipline that Merton recommended in the beginning of his teaching on prayer in the early sixties, but also so that the ability to choose can separate you, can take you, so that you can bring together your own self, your own choice, your own inner self-being and choose according to that rather than what somebody else tells you or influences you or says you should be doing.

And how important that is for us in our times. Merton saw it, and he talked a lot about alienation, about the split between our true self and the self we put onto us, the ballast we've taken on, the false self, the self that somebody else has decided what we should do. Deciding ourselves what we should do and how to do it, true choice is what Merton is up to so much in the very last months of his life. As you read the Alaskan journal,[22] what Merton said in Alaska, and the conferences he gave, you will see this coming out more and more, as well as in the final talk[23] where he talks about alienation, to such an extent that we can see that it has something to do with the true self, the false self, the true self being the deep self living in union with God or living in the presence of God or living and making decisions in that presence, and the false self, that is, what we have taken on from somebody else.

I'd like to teach you a little Sufi song: "Who is in my temple? All the doors do open themselves. All the lights do light themselves. Darkness like a dark bird, flies away, flies away." The word *who* is a very important word in the Islamic tradition, especially in the Sufi tradition. Here it refers to God. So when I say WHO is in my temple, that's what I'm really saying. Who is in my temple? Who is in my temple? All the doors open themselves. It is not done by me. The doors are open, themselves. They are opened for me. All the doors are open themselves. All the lights light themselves. All the wonderful things that happen happen not because I make them. The lights light themselves. And when that happens, then darkness like a dark bird flies away, flies away. So it is a beautiful little Sufi thing that we can bring right into our own life and see it as a Christian thing, as a different approach, certainly.

In the last part of this little talk we'll talk about Merton and prayer towards the very end of Merton's life. He was growing in all kinds of ways and turned to the presence of the East that he so often read about and so long read about, and here he was treasuring these moments with the Dalai Lama, with other great experts in Buddhism and Hinduism, and approaching what he was going to have after the next month, in Japan with the Buddhists. He never reached there, as you know, but at least he was on his way to as much as he could learn about God's manifestation to everything in being.[24]

It seems to me the great part of his kind of insight is that we see how God has been present to every human being, and that's the beauty of it, I think. That's the love part of it—that God thought to create each one of us. I was saying this to a group last summer, and so I asked the question: What does that say about baptism and so forth? A priest who was in the group raised his hand and said, "The fact is that God is present to every single human being radically and freely and in the fullest absolute way." He made the comment which was very insightful, I thought: "Baptism is the celebration and formalization of that truth." And to me that was a marvelous way to put it. Baptism brings one into the circle of the faithful who can learn the message of Jesus Christ in a real and true way, but the reality is already there, so celebrate it. We have the sacraments of the church to bring us within the Christian community into a way that that's possible.

What was Merton saying and doing the last few months of his life? Many people say to me, "Well, you know he had that beautiful experience at Polannaruwa in Sri Lanka, and he stood there in the presence of the great Buddhas and explained with joy how the aesthetical and the spiritual came together for him in that marvelous experience of Polannaruwa."[25] And he talked to people about that, and I think they did not understand him as maybe we don't. I have had people say to me, "Well, isn't it too bad that his last vision of greatness wasn't in a Catholic church somewhere?" And I think well now look—don't miss the point. Of course, Catholic church, of course, all of it, but it so happened to Merton who was speaking for the way God manifests God's self in all. That happened to him there, that he saw the whole thing come together in one marvelous insight. It was all okay. He said, "Witness the beauty of what I've come to Asia to learn. I know it. I know that all is one. The marvelous revelation that has been given to all of us is manifested to me in this particular Asian garden."

And it seems to me that this is what should pull us out, expanding ourselves into much more than the narrowness that we might otherwise have. When Merton was moving through this period, and moving through the last part of his life, he was continually able to say these things to the people around him. He has many illustrations of it. And he continued to see how the way of learning this comes through the appreciation of God's gifts to us. You know, I'm sure, the beautiful prayer where Merton writes to a Sufi and the Sufi asks him how he himself prays.[26] Now from what I've said before you certainly understand that Merton was not fond of talking about himself and how he prayed. And so when Abdul Aziz, the great learned Sufi man, wrote to him and said, "How do you pray?" Merton resisted it and didn't answer him, and it was only after some time that Abdul Aziz goes back to him and says, "You didn't tell me everything. I want to know more." And so Aziz says, "Well, I want to know how *you* pray." Merton had no alternative then but to answer. So he does it in a very simple way. He says, "Well, this is the way I pray."

Then Merton gives a little sketch of how he himself prays and he puts it this way: "Now you ask about my method of meditation. Strictly speaking I have a very simple way of prayer. [Wouldn't you know it—from all he said through the years—very simple.] It is centered entirely on attention to the presence of God and to His will and His love. That is to say that it is centered on *faith* by which alone one can know the presence of God." [One is aware of this gift by accepting it as the presence of God. One becomes aware of it through faith.] Only through faith, says Merton, can we say that the presence of God is known. Now notice how Merton uses "faith" not just as dogmas or belief systems but as this profound sense of each one of us who are before God. That is how he is looking at faith here. "One might say this gives my meditation the character described by the Prophet as 'being before God as if you saw him.'"[27]

Often when I am reading with a group I'll say, "Who does Merton mean by 'the prophet'?" Some will say "Isaiah," and some will say somebody else, and finally someone will always say "Muhammed." And the reason they will always say "Muhammed" as the prophet is that Merton is respectfully talking to a Sufi; he is talking to a man for whom the words of Muhammed were the words of *the* prophet. Now Merton doesn't say, "Now I will tell you why Muhammed doesn't have the last word." Merton doesn't say any of that. Merton is respectful of God's revelation to every person in every age, and he respects Muhammed and therefore says to the Sufi, "the words of the prophet," and he doesn't say *"your prophet";* he says "the *words of the prophet.*" When Merton says *"kneeling before God,"* he is very respectful of the Sufi's own words. Yet it does not mean anything, Merton says, like conceiving a precise image of God. That would be a kind of idolatry.[28] On the contrary, it is knowing [God] as the invisible beyond our comprehension, and realizing God as all.

Recently I read that beautiful description that Albert Einstein gave when somebody asked him what was his religiousness. Einstein, from a totally different religious background, said, "My religiousness consists in this: I stand in humble admiration before the infinite superior spirit who revealed the little that we with our weak and transitory understanding can comprehend of reality." Beautiful sense of a great scientist. "I stand in humble admiration before the infinite superior spirit who reveals the little we can take in because our understanding is weak and transitory." Who reveals the little we can understand of the ultimate reality? And for anybody who is following me so far, you can see how this simply enlarges and makes even greater the understanding of God's presence to each one of us.

Merton goes on then and says, "My prayer is then a kind of praise rising up out of the center of Nothing and Silence."[29] Merton was, of course, sure that God is all, and we are nothing. And unless you understand the *"all is God"* and *"we are nothing"* part of it, you don't understand what Merton is talking about at all. Because of the *"we are nothing,"* we are the incredible hosts of God, but of ourselves we are nothing. We didn't bring any of it with us into the world. Open the hand of the newborn baby, and there is nothing there. All is gift; everything there, the gifts of faith and so on, and unless we understand that, we will not know what is meant by *"God is all, and we are nothing."* But he knew that, and therefore when he prayed he was conscious of it and really that it is all a gift of faith.

Merton goes on from that and finally thanked the Sufi and tells him to be discreet about this. Merton wants Aziz to adore God, praise God, pray to God for the world which is in great trouble and confusion, never separating the word from the world. And he says he will be with him this month of Ramadan.[30] We must think about that when we get into the month of Ramadan that is coming. Then I will be with you, and I appreciate the Sufi tradition, and I will remember you on the Night of Destiny…. Then Merton concludes by saying "May the Most High God [which again is an expression of Islam] send His blessing upon you and give you peace." [31]

So Merton in his great charity prays openly with all religions and expresses this beautifully within his own Christian context. And I think that is what we need to do. We need to be stretched by Merton, and we can be stretched if we take something very seriously about his journey, his journey that never abandoned the core that I began in the beginning to express to you: God's true reality, presence that is more than presence, a reality within us, which God has graciously given us at the core of what it was all about. If we identify it ourselves that way, then we have the doors opened for us. And Merton does that in all that he says.

I want to conclude by telling you about Merton's last words. Merton gave a talk in Bangkok, a final contribution, and he talked quite a bit about alienation,[32] the separation of ourselves, tearing ourselves into two parts: that which somebody else tells us we are, and that which we know ourselves to be as a center where God is present. Now if we choose from that center, as Merton continually instructed his novices, then we are choosing according to a unified sense of self. If we choose from what other people tell us we are or tell us we should do, or tell us anything else that we should do, or have or whatever, we have broken ourselves into two. That's alienation. And that's what Merton talked about so much in his last days, that alienated self, brought all the way over to what others say we should be rather than choosing from one's center. That is what I think was the great message of prayer and everything else that Merton taught. At the end of it he asked for the blessing of God for himself and for all these others that are there.

In the very last of his life, he gave this final talk in Bangkok. I went to the place in Bangkok, and I visited the room where he gave the final talk, and I visited the little bungalow where he died. I remembered then what I heard about his last words. Merton, as you know, gave his talk, and then sat down and said, "We are going to have the questions tonight. Now I will disappear." [33] Many people repeat that as a prophecy. I don't really think it was prophecy. I think Merton meant he'd leave. And we'll have the questions tonight.

So then he went from there to the lunchroom and had the lunch they had prepared, and then he walked over to his room accompanied by a French monk[34] who talked to him as they walked along to Merton's room and said to him, "Well, thank you for the talk you gave this morning. Everybody didn't exactly appreciate it, though. We had some questions." And I thought to myself, "Yes, this is the way it always is. Yes, I know they said some good things BUT." There's always that little part, and Merton was experiencing that there. Actually, it was a nun that said that, but usually I don't say that because we have a bad enough press as it is, so I don't usually set up the nun as the one who said that. Anyone could have. She happened to say it, and what she said was repeated to Merton: "I thought he would talk more about converting people to Christianity. I thought that's what he was going to be talking about." She enlarged on that. This is a pagan area where we are working, and we're missionaries, and it's a pagan area, and here he's talking about something else and alienation, whatever. But I thought he'd talk about bringing people to Christ.

Merton, when he heard that, instead of getting upset the way many of us would get upset, said simply, "Well, I don't think that is what we are asked to do today. All the preaching we get on television telling us who God is—honestly, you wonder what the word 'God' is to mean in all of that." Merton has it better. "Today I don't think it is what we are asked to do. I think today it's more important for us to so let God live in us that others may feel God and come to believe in God because they feel how God lives in us." These were Merton's last words that we know anything about and were said right before François de Grunne took him to his room where he tragically died, tragically for us, in any case. Certainly he had completed what was his journey. In other words, so let God live in us, so allow God to be the center where we make our decisions, where we live our lives, so let God live in us that others may find God by seeing how God lives in us, by somehow grasping how God lives in us. Better than any long television explanation of who God is. A beautiful last message, and I'd like to leave that with you as we conclude the talk on prayer because prayer, that presence of God, that reality of God, which each of us possesses, is our good fortune, "All love's luck." We have achieved it. Thank you very much.

Endnotes

1. "Prayer and Commitment" is a talk given by Mary Luke Tobin at Nazareth College, Rochester, New York, on November 3, 1990, at a program entitled: "A Day on Thomas Merton with Sister Mary Luke Tobin."

2. *Freedom in Exile: The Autobiography of the Dalai Lama* (New York: Harper Collins, 1990).

3. For accounts of that meeting see N. Burton, P. Hart, J. Laughlin, eds, "The Himalayas" in *The Asian Journal of Thomas Merton* (New York: New Directions, 1968/75), 77-190, Harold Talbott's reflections in Bonnie Thurston, ed., *Merton and Buddhism* (Louisville: Fons Vitae, 2007), 224-232, and the interview with Talbott, "The Jesus Lama: Thomas Merton in the Himalayas," *Tricycle: The Buddhist Review* (Summer, 1992), 14-24.

4. *Freedom in Exile*, 189.

5. Ibid.

6. Ibid.

7. Ibid., 189-190.

8. These ideas are found in chapters 5 and 6 of *New Seeds of Contemplation* (New York: New Directions, 1961) where Merton says, "God utters me like a word containing a partial thought of Himself," 37.

9. Robert Daggy was, at the time, director of the Thomas Merton Studies Center, Bellarmine University, Louisville, Ky.

10. Merton's journal entries of April 11 and April 22, 1951, focus on Fr. Charbel. See Jonathan Montaldo, ed. *Entering the Silence: The Journals of Thomas Merton* Volume Two 1941-1952 (San Francisco: Harper San Francisco, 1996), 454-457.

11. In Jane Marie Richardson, SL, ed., *The Springs of Contemplation* (New York: Farrar, Straus, Giroux, 1992), ix.

12. Paul Pearson reports this quotation is from the preface Merton wrote to "Selections on Prayer," a collection of writing about prayer Merton compiled for the choir novitiate in Lent 1961. The exact quotation is "Prayer is not only the 'lifting up of the mind and heart to God,' but it is also the response to God within us, the discovery of God within us; it leads ultimately to the discovery and fulfillment of our own true being in God."

13. On October 15, 1961, Merton describes his joy in a visit to Loretto. See Victor A. Kramer, ed. *Turning Toward the World: The Journals of Thomas Merton* Volume Four 1960-1963 (San Francisco: Harper San Francisco, 1997), 167-168. The same volume reports a visit on October 2, 1960, 54.

14. The text of this letter appears in Br. Patrick Hart, OCSO, ed., *Thomas Merton, The School of Charity* (New York: Farrar, Straus, Giroux, 1990), 140-141.

15. Merton includes this quotation from Dom Chapman in his journal entry of September 13, 1949. Jonathan Montaldo (ed.), *Entering the Silence* Journals of Thomas Merton (1941–1952) (San Francisco: Harper San Francisco, 1996), 367.

16. See May 15, 1963, Talk to Novices and Postulants in Part I of this book.

17. *New Seeds of Contemplation*. The passage Luke alludes to is on p. 3.

18. Merton also spoke of these ideas in "Contemporary Prophetic Choices"

(1967) and "Contemplative Life as Prophetic Vocation," "Prophecy, Alienation, Language" (both 1968) in *The Springs of Contemplation*.

19. For more see James S. Cutsinger, ed., *Paths to the Heart: Sufism and the Christian East* (Louisville: Fons Vitae, 2002) and B. Dieker and J. Montaldo, eds., *Merton and Hesychasm: The Prayer of the Heart* (Louisville: Fons Vitae, 2003).

20. For more see R. Baker and G. Henry, eds., *Merton and Sufism* (Louisville: Fons Vitae, 1999). Some of the material that follows here is also found in Bernadette Dieker, "Merton's Sufi Lectures to Cistercian Novices, 1966-68" in *Merton and Hesychasm,* 130-162.

21. See, for example, "Prophecy, Alienation, Language" in *The Springs of Contemplation*.

22. *Thomas Merton in Alaska* (New York: New Directions, 1988).

23. "Marxism and Monastic Perspectives," December 10, 1968. It appears in *The Asian Journal of Thomas Merton,* 326-343.

24. Sr. Luke here alludes to Merton's time in Asia, roughly from October to December 10, 1968.

25. The experience is recounted in *The Asian Journal of Thomas Merton,* 230-236.

26. The letter appears in William H. Shannon, ed., *Thomas Merton, The Hidden Ground of Love: Letters* (NY: Farrar, Straus, Giroux, 1985), 62-64.

27. Ibid., 63.

28. Ibid., 63-64. Idolatry (*shirk*) is Islam's cardinal sin.

29. Ibid., 64.

30. The Islamic month of fasting.

31. *Hidden Ground*, 64.

32. The text of the talk is printed in *The Asian Journal of Thomas Merton*, Appendix vii, 326-343.

33. The exact words were: "I believe the plan is to have all the questions... this evening at the panel. So I will disappear." *The Asian Journal of Thomas Merton*, 343.

34. The monk in question was Dom François de Grunne, OSB.

Part III: A Portrait of Loretto
and Faces of Wisdom

*The bell tower at Loretto Motherhouse*

*The mission bell at Loretto, rung when sisters departed for foreign missions and on other special occasions*

*Mary's Lake*

*Fr. Nerinckx's cabin, moved from "Little Loretto" near St. Charles, KY, site of the community's foundation*

*Winter scene at Loretto*

*Inside Loretto Motherhouse church*

*Pieta Chapel, with a Pieta painting Fr. Nerinckx brought from Europe in the early 1800s*

*Mary Luke Tobin with Cardinal Joseph E. Ritter in Rome during Vatican Council II*

*Mary Luke Tobin, Mary Florence Wolff, SL, and Mary Benedicta, OP, with Cardinal Leon Joseph Suenens at Mundelein College, Chicago, 1963*

*Luke is greeted by Rose Maureen Sanders, SL, (Helen after 1970) on Luke's return from a Vatican Council session*

*Cao Ngoc Phuong, Thich Nhat Hanh, Luke, and Dorothy Cotton of Southern Christian Leadership Con-ference at Citizens' Conference on Ending the War in Indochina, Paris, March, 1971*

*Luke during meeting of the International Thomas Merton Society, Colorado Springs, 1993*

*Luke and Cecily Jones, SL, at a demonstration for equality of women in the Roman Catholic Church, mid-1990s, Denver*

*Luke receiving the US Catholic award for "Furthering the Cause of Women in the Church," 1986*

*Luke speaking at workshop on "Collaborative Witness of Women and Men in the Church," sponsored by Glenmary, 1985*

*Luke at Ring Lake Ranch, Dubois, WY, where she was guest lecturer for 15 summers*

*Patrick Hart, OCSO, and Luke at Gethsemani*

*Rose Alma Schuler, SL, and Luke. Rose Alma was Loretto secretary general, 1958-70, when Luke was superior general.*

*Luke and Agnes Cecile Siefert, SL, at their 75th jubilee as Sisters of Loretto, December 8, 2002*

*Luke and Jane Marie Richardson, SL, who was on the Loretto General Council with Luke, 1964-70 and editor of The Springs of Contemplation.*

*Jeanne Dueber, SL, sculptor, at Mary's Lake*

*Antoinette Doyle, SL*

*Samina Iqbal, SL, Maria Daniel, SL, and Iffat Peter, SL, the youngest Sisters of Loretto, now in Pakistan*

*Jane Frances Mueller, SL*

*Carol Dunphy, SL, Cecily Jones, and Luke, 2004. These three and two others lived together for many years in Denver.*

*Mary Swain, SL*

*Marie Therese Koch, SL, celebrating her 100th birthday*

*Pauline Albin, SL*

*Helen Jean Seidel, SL, novice director when Luke was superior general*

*Cathy Mueller, SL, president of Loretto, 2007-2012, and Susan Swain, SL, Loretto leadership group, 2000-2009.*

*Elizabeth Dacanay, SL, Patricia Jean Manion, SL, Matthew Geraghty, SL, and Christina Cheng, SL. Elizabeth and Christina attended the Loretto school in Shanghai; Matthew taught there; and PJ wrote the story of Loretto in China in* Venture into the Unknown.

*Alicia Ramirez, SL*

*Mary Frances Lottes, SL, on the Loretto General Council with Luke, 1964-70, and Kathleen Vonderhaar, SL. Both have been involved in working with the inmates at Marion County Detention Center.*

*Anthony Mary Sartorius, SL, and Michaela Collins, SL*

*Luke, clockwise starting upper left: 1969, 1980, 1997, 1993*

*Written about a year before the close of Luke's earthly life, this poem captures the poignant contrast betwee*
*her former vibrant self and her now frail response to her surroundings. The poet, Luke's friend of many yea*
*delights in knowing that nature's gifts and even such mundane objects as gravel trucks help awaken Luk*
*attention. Her world of exchanging ideas has been replaced by a different kind of dialog.*

# The World Beyond Your Window
(for Luke)

The world beyond your window
has so comforted my heart this year
that I bless each truck, tree, and bird
I see out there, bless them for their being
and bless them for that pique of interest in your eyes.

We watched expansion trundled in
and counted gravel trucks to twelve.
Who'd think the rollered spread of tar
or a parking line machine
could be the lore for conversation?

The world beyond your window
revealed tiny chartreuse finches
at the feeder. And now we marvel
at the swirling fog swallowing the dawn
and hint of scarlet tinting maple leaves.

When others ask if you converse
I want to say *of course*,
pretending that your nodded *yes*,
your phrases left mid-voice,
your gentle pointing at a puff of cloud
create the stuff of deepest dialog.

My dear, I yearn to hear you read
some lines from Levertov or Rumi,
Rahner, Merton, your recent Oliver.
I miss the charge of searching energy,
the delve and questioning, the lifted hope,
but, suddenly engulfed in grace, I bless
the marigolds and barn you see as you embrace
the world beyond your window.

— Cecily Jones, SL

*Luke in the 1990s*

*Burying the cremains of Luke and of Helen Sanders, in Loretto cemetery, May 16, 2008, Luke's 100th birthday. Cecily with shovel, Rose Alma Schuler and Carol Dunphy in wheelchairs, Elaine Prevallet, SL offering a prayer*

# Permissions/Acknowledgements/Thanksgivings

## Permissions/Acknowledgements

The Merton Legacy Trust gave permission to publish the edited transcripts of three talks Thomas Merton gave to the novices of the Sisters of Loretto and his "Comments on the Vows."

Farrar, Straus and Giroux, Inc., gave permission to reprint "Loretto and Gethsemani," which appeared in Jane Marie Richardson, ed., *The Springs of Contemplation* (New York: Farrar, Straus, Giroux, 1992).

Farrar, Straus and Giroux, Inc. also gave permission to reprint the two letters from 1962 which appeared in William H. Shannon, ed., *Thomas Merton, Witness to Freedom: Letters in Times of Crisis* (New York: Farrar, Straus, Giroux, 1994).

Permission was sought from Credence Cassettes to publish the transcript of the tape *Prayer and Commitment in Thomas Merton*. It was not possible to make contact by e-mail, fax, or telephone.

In general, permissions were sought, and any omissions will be acknowledged in future editions.

## Thanksgivings

### General Editor

Perhaps the general editor speaks for us all when she admits to having a "Horton the Elephant" tenacity about this book which was begun in 2001, drafted in 2003 and now, finally, is in print. In *Horton Hatches the Egg*, Dr. Seuss' elephant, Horton, constantly repeats, "I meant what I said/ And I said what I meant/ An elephant's faithful/ One hundred percent!" We have been faithful to Sr. Mary Luke Tobin and brought her book into being, no one more so than Sr. Mary Swain, SL, whose cheerful and patient tenacity has achieved so much for us. Br. Paul Quenon, OCSO, has been our artistic voice, and Gray Henry and Neville Blakemore at Fons Vitae have pulled the work together with characteristic attention. Thanks, many thanks to them and to Sr. Rose Annette Liddell, SL, who kept nudging me to get to the editing, and Sr. Mary Catherine Rabbitt, SL, then president of the Loretto community, who in 2002 gave the work the go-ahead. Thanks to all the Sisters of Loretto who contributed their memory and time to this project. Paul Pearson checked many references for us and is, as always, the master of things Mertonian. Patrick F. O'Connell's eagle eye saved us many an error. Anne McCormick was invaluable in the securing of permissions and thanks are due through her to the Merton Legacy Trust. But my greatest gratitude goes to Sr. Luke for her friendship over many years and for the insistence that this work had the continued relevance that it does. To all these and several more who prefer not to be named, I am most grateful.

Loretto Editor

My thanks go to Bonnie Thurston for her scholarship, devotion, and diligence in making this book possible. Thanks, too, to Neville Blakemore at Fons Vitae for his craftsmanship, evident in the book itself, and to Gray Henry at Fons Vitae who somehow made sure this book was published.

Thanks to Paul Pearson for so promptly finding references for us, and to Anita Johnson, Head of Public Services, Clifford E. Barbour Library, Pittsburgh Theological Seminary, and William Kevin Cawley, Archivist, Notre Dame University, for locating dates of publication for us.

I am also grateful to Anne McCormick of the Merton Legacy Trust for her guiding me along with knowledge and ease.

Others who made the publication of this book possible are Cecily Jones, SL, Peg Jacobs, CoL, Paul Quenon, OCSO, James Conner, OCSO, and Patrick O'Connell.

Gethsemani Photography Editor

Thanks to the spirit of adventure that wildly inspired Gray Henry, Eleanor Bingham Miller and me. After these women bravely climbed the vertical ladder inside of Gethsemani's bell tower 50 feet to the top, we crawled through the hatch onto the roof of the church, and sat to rest. There the scheme was hatched to expand Bonnie Thurston's introduction and transcription into a book size collection, with photographs and related items.

*Close-up of door hinge in Loretto novitiate building*